MODERN CALIFORNIA POLITICS

MODERN CALIFORNIA POLITICS

1917 - 1980

Jackson K. Putnam

series editors:
Norris Hundley, jr.
John A. Schutz

Boyd & Fraser Publishing Company
San Francisco

MODERN CALIFORNIA POLITICS

Jackson K. Putnam

© copyright 1980 by Boyd & Fraser Publishing Company, 3627 Sacramento Street, San Francisco, CA 94118. All rights reserved.

Manufactured in the United States of America.

Library of Congress catalog card number: 80-80026

ISBN 0-87835-096-9

2 3 4 5 · 4 3 2 1 0

EDITORS' INTRODUCTION

MENTION THE NAME CALIFORNIA and the popular mind conjures up images of romance and adventure of the sort that prompted the Spaniards in the 1540s to name the locale after a legendary Amazon queen. State of mind no less than geographic entity, California has become a popular image of a wonderful land of easy wealth, better health, pleasant living, and unlimited opportunities. While this has been true for some, for others it has been a land of disillusionment, and for too many it has become a place of crowded cities, congested roadways, smog, noise, racial unrest, and other problems. Still, the romantic image has persisted to make California the most populated state in the Union and the home of more newcomers each year than came during the first three hundred years following discovery by Europeans.

For most of its history California has been shrouded in mystery, better known for its terrain than for its settlers—first the Indians who arrived at least 11,000 years ago and then the Spaniards who followed in 1769. Spaniards, Mexicans, and blacks added only slightly to the non-Indian population until the American conquest of 1846 ushered in an era of unparalleled growth. With the discovery of gold, the building of the transcontinental railroad, and the development of crops and cities, people in massive numbers from all parts of the world began to inhabit the region. Thus California became a land of newcomers where a rich mixture of cultures pervades.

Fact and fiction are intertwined so well into the state's traditions and folklore that they are sometimes difficult to separate. But close scrutiny reveals that the people of California have made many solid contributions in land and water use, conservation of resources, politics, education, transportation, labor organization, literature, architectural styles, and learning to live with people of different cultural and ethnic heritages. These contributions, as well as those instances when Californians performed less admirably, are woven into the design of the Golden

State Series. The volumes in the Series are meant to be suggestive rather than exhaustive, interpretive rather than definitive. They invite the general public, the student, the scholar, and the teacher to read them not only for digested materials from a wide range of recent scholarship, but also for some new insights and ways of perceiving old problems. The Series, we trust, will be only the beginning of each reader's inquiry into the past of a state rich in historical excitement and significant in its impact on the nation.

Norris Hundley, jr.
John A. Schutz

CONTENTS

CHAPTER ONE

The 1920s: Origins of the Modern Era

C ALIFORNIA POLITICS of the last sixty years is largely the product of the Progressive movement. The California brand of this nationwide, urban, middle-class crusade was led by Governor Hiram Johnson, a moralistic and pragmatic reformer who sought to purify the political process, which allegedly had been corrupted by big business, and to rescue the victims of social injustice whose plight also seemed mainly the fault of big business. Coming to power in 1911, Johnson and his Progressive followers set about achieving political reform by taking power away from corrupt political machines financed by business corporations, especially the Southern Pacific Railroad, and placing it in the hands of "the people." Their chosen devices for doing this included the direct primary, woman's suffrage, the initiative, referendum, and recall, nonpartisan local elections, and cross-filing. Socioeconomic reform was brought about through banking and public utility regulation, a rash of labor and welfare legislation, especially establishing a worker's compensation system, the passage of various aid-to-agriculture legislation, and the enactment of several laws to conserve natural resources and to protect the environment.

In a mere half-dozen years the Progressives wrote most of their program into law, and California politics is still profoundly affected by their labors. Although historians today strenuously debate the effectiveness and impact of their reforms, it seems safe to say that they established a tradition of honest, relatively nonpartisan government, conservative enough to recognize the merits of industrial capitalism but liberal enough to perceive its flaws, and humane enough to work for the correction of social injustices in defiance of the strictures of the ideology of *laissez faire*. In short, the modern California political arena in which the liberal, practical, reform politician contends with his conservative, *laissez faire*, doctrinaire opponent was mainly constructed during the Progressive era, and to a considerable extent this arena is still intact.

On March 15, 1917, Hiram Johnson left the state in a huff. Newly elected to the United States Senate, he bitterly believed that his successor as governor was a cold-hearted "man without a soul" who would preside over the destruction of the Progressive movement and deliver California into the hands of the reactionaries. Many historians tend to agree with Johnson that a decline of progressivism was indeed the primary product of William D. Stephens's governorship, but they tend to blame Johnson as much as Stephens for the misfortune. Overly sensitive, undiplomatic, and pugnacious, Johnson made enemies out of many of his closest supporters, especially in the southern part of the state, and he himself was largely responsible for the disarray of the Progressive coalition at the time of his departure. Furthermore, many say the times destroyed the Progressive movement more than the deliberate actions of politicians. The reform spirit had largely run its course by 1917, it is said, and entry into World War I destroyed what remained of it. Stephens, according to this argument, was "bum-rapped" by Johnson for supposedly causing something that no one could have prevented.

The trouble with this argument is that it begs the main question. The first question for the student of modern California politics is: "What happened to the Progressive movement in California after the Johnson era?" Contrary to the common opinion of many authorities, there is reason to believe that progressivism was not killed by the war but, like many veterans of that disaster, lived on for many years and in a sense is still alive today. William D. Stephens, according to this view, should be regarded as the savior of progressivism, not its destroyer, not merely the hapless and ineffectual successor of Hiram Johnson but a successful and significant political leader in his own right.

Who was William D. Stephens? Colorless but competent, perhaps he might better be described as a typical southern Californian. Like many of his counterparts he migrated to Los Angeles from the Midwest (Ohio) in the great boom year of 1887. Entering the grocery business he soon prospered and became prominent in civic affairs. A church-going, teetotaling member of the Shrine and Masonic brotherhoods and a leading figure in the Los Angeles Chamber of Commerce, he gravitated naturally into the local "Good Government" movement. A member of the advisory boards that brought about two of the growing city's greatest and most controversial achievements— the Los Angeles Harbor and the Owens River Aqueduct—he was chosen as interim mayor in the famous recall campaign of 1909 when the badly compromised incumbent Mayor A. C. Harper deprived his constituents of the pleasure of recalling him by resigning two weeks before the election. Like his reform colleagues Stephens joined the statewide Lincoln-Roosevelt League, which endorsed him as Republican candidate for the United States House of Representatives in 1910. Sharing in the great Progressive sweep of that year which put Hiram Johnson in the State House, he won election and was reelected on the Republican ticket in 1912 and as a Progressive in 1914. When Hiram Johnson decided to run for the U.S. Senate in 1916 and when his hand-picked successor, Lieutenant Governor Fred Eshelman, died suddenly in office, the southern California Progressive contingent forced Johnson to choose Stephens as acting lieutenant governor and thus governor if Johnson should be elected to the Senate. It was the victorious Johnson's strange suspicion that Stephens was a false Progressive that led to his ludicrous decision to delay his resignation as governor to the last possible moment. Despite the bruised feelings and intra-party abrasions that followed, Stephens held much of the Progressive coalition together through the remainder of Johnson's unexpired term and was elected governor in his own right in 1918 despite Johnson's covert opposition.[1]

But was his administration a triumph for progressivism or for reaction? Perhaps the fairest answer to this question would be that it was a bit of both. From the viewpoint of doctrinaire liberals there was reaction enough. Convinced with many others that a dangerous radical conspiracy led by the Industrial Workers of the World (IWW) and other "disloyal" and "violent" elements was taking place in America, Stephens, capitalizing on his well cultivated stance as a war governor, called for strong legislative action to deal with the "red menace." The result was the passage of the Criminal Syndicalism Act of 1919. This notorious law, which authorized the state to prosecute individuals and organizations for their expressed beliefs rather than their actions, enabled California to break up the IWW and harry dozens of individuals into prison over the next generation, but like the federal government's famous "red raids" of the same time, more damage was probably done to the U.S. Constitution and the civil rights of individuals than to America's enemies real or imagined. The governor has also been faulted for refusing to pardon or secure a new trial for the famous labor "martyrs" Thomas Mooney and Warren Billings after it became apparent that their conviction of murder in the sensational Preparedness Day bombing incident of 1916 had been a flagrant miscarriage of justice. Furthermore, it is alleged that the antiradical campaign became in reality an antilabor campaign, with unions becoming discredited in the public mind as disloyal and un-American, a stigma that remained with them and contributed to their decline throughout the decade of the 1920s. Stephens's veto of the Flaherty anti-injunction bill in 1917 to protect legitimate unions from hostile state actions allegedly contributed to this atmosphere and showed the governor's unfriendliness to the labor movement.

More damaging to Stephens's reputation than the red-baiting charge is the allegation that he was a race bigot as well. Not only a "red menace" but a "yellow peril," he insisted, was threatening the state. At first reluctant to support the renewed outbreaks of virulent anti-Japanese hysteria sweeping the state in 1919, he soon joined the ranks of the Japanese exclusionists by releasing a highly biased official state report, *California and the Oriental,* which purported to prove that the Japanese population in the state (about two percent of the total) threatened to engulf the

Caucasian element in the next generation or two! He also endorsed the alien land initiative of 1920, which was ineffectual in slowing the growth of Japanese land ownership but highly fruitful in producing hostility and ill will on both the local and international scenes. Not surprisingly Stephens also subscribed to the notion prevailing among anti-Orientalists that the only workable solution to the problem was for the federal government to halt the migration of Japanese nationals to the country, and he was characteristically pleased when the Congress adopted that course in the Immigration Act of 1924.

Finally, Stephens has been faulted for his support of the prohibition movement. A long-time "dry," he had voted for the Eighteenth Amendment to the U.S. Constitution[2] while a member of Congress and urged the state legislature to ratify it, which it did in 1919. He also supported the passage of two prohibition enforcement acts which defined intoxicating beverages in the same way as the federal government's stringent Volstead Act. Both acts have come to be regarded as ineffectual travesties of any sane principles of law enforcement because they failed to reduce alcoholic consumption, encouraged professional hoodlums and law-breaking by honest citizens, and seriously interfered with individual privacy and basic human rights. Despite the obvious failure of the law, prohibitionists continued to dominate the legislature until 1932, and refused to countenance any suggestion of its repeal or modification.

Despite these damning indictments there is considerable to be said on Stephens's behalf. If the Criminal Syndicalism Act is indefensible,[3] the fear of radicalism was not. The governor's executive mansion was bombed while Stephens was living in it; a bomb addressed to him was intercepted in a San Francisco post office; and he received an extortion letter threatening further bombings if a $50,000 payment were not made. Though he refused to free Mooney and Billings, he did save their lives, first by postponing their death sentences and then by commuting them to life imprisonment despite his personal belief that they were guilty as charged. Though he vetoed the Flaherty bill, he secured the passage of other prolabor legislation, such as that providing for vocational rehabilitation for industrial accident victims and enforcing wages and hours legislation for women and minorities. Though the Flaherty veto angered the unions, his veto of a trading stamp bill in 1917 earned him the animosity of the mercantile interests, just as his appointments to the Railroad Commission angered many public utilities companies. Though Stephens's record on the Japanese question is reprehensible, it is well to remember that the California Progressives had always been bigots on the issue, and in other racial affairs his record appears more enlightened. The 1919 legislature passed a law, which he signed, prohibiting racial discrimination in public places, and when the Ku Klux Klan raised its ugly head in the state, the governor forbade state employees to join it. Finally, prohibition had long been favored by many Progressives; it did attempt to deal with a widely acknowledged set of social, economic, and political evils; and its weaknesses and failures only became apparent long after Stephens was out of office.

Perhaps more significant than the qualifications that can be placed on Stephens's progressive failures is the fact that he has many positive progressive achievements to his credit as well. If the main thrust of progressivism was to establish governmental agencies to regulate interest groups (particularly businesses) in behalf of the public at large and to protect certain classes of citizens (women, children, the aged, the infirm, and others), then this process continued apace during the Stephens administration. One student calculates the total number of such new services during Stephens's tenure at 59, with 31 created in a single legislative session (1921), a record performance for any administration including Hiram Johnson's. While much of this record can be regarded as simply a continuation of the Progressive momentum engendered during the Johnson era (the ratification of the Nineteenth Amendment to the U.S. Constitution providing for women's suffrage in 1919 might be an example), other actions taken seem more innovative and original. In resource development, the state's hard-surface highway system was established with the passage of a $40,000,000 bond issue in 1919, and Stephens attempted to do somewhat the same thing with the state's water resources. A measure of state control over irrigation and hydroelectric power projects was gained in 1919 and 1921, and Stephens sought to inaugurate the comprehensive Central Valley Project proposed by the U.S. Bureau of Reclamation, but was frustrated by the private power companies

whose massive attacks upon the program as "socialism" persuaded the voters to reject it in 1922.

But Stephens's greatest claims to fame as a Progressive lay in
the fields of fiscal policy and government management. Despite
the conservative cries for governmental retrenchment and economy which began to fill the air after World War I, Stephens unabashedly proposed an expansion of state spending and a tax
increase to finance it. Since the tax proposal embodied in the so-
called King Bill of 1921 called for a 35 percent increase in
corporation taxes, it brought out the "billion dollar lobby" in
full force in a vain effort to defeat it. The passage of the law
enabled Stephens to increase the state's biennial budget by
more than 50 percent, and, although this too was bitterly opposed by fiscal conservatives, the new budget passed easily.
Such a record would seem to make Stephens highly vulnerable
to charges of being a fiscally irresponsible spendthrift politician,
but the wily governor was busily protecting himself against this
attack as well. By consolidating the several dozen governmental
agencies and commissions into five centrally organized departments on the model of the large business corporation, Stephens
could, and did, claim that he was not an old-school politician but
a modern "business manager" whose watchwords were efficiency
and responsibility. With an improved budgeting and accounting
system also to his credit, with his constant calls for efficiency
and economy on the part of administrators and legislators, and
with frequent vetoes of bills whose objectives he approved of
but which he thought the state could not afford, he projected an
image of the pragmatic administrator rather than the irresponsible bureaucrat.

In fact, if one word could characterize what progressivism had
become under Stephens, that word would be "pragmatic." Although originating as basically a moral philosophy of what was
good and true in politics, progressivism had become a practical
philosophy of what was politically and economically possible.
Originally a political ideology in which public policies were
adopted on the basis of supposedly fundamental principles of
right and wrong, it now sought to apply such principles in the
context of what the situation would allow. Any such situation,
furthermore, had often been found to be much more complex

than the simple ideological notions that were supposed to
"cover" it, and it became necessary to study the situation closely
before devising policies to deal with it. Even then, a policy
might or might not work, and trial and error became a necessary and desirable governmental tactic. Stephens devised most
of his major policies, "good" and "bad," only after he had
appointed governmental commissions to make detailed studies
of the problem, and he made his decisions not only on the basis
of what the studies revealed but also upon the political atmosphere of the times. Although Governor Johnson before him had
actually begun this policy shift in the direction of pragmatism,
Stephens carried it further and made it a cardinal principle of
administrative policy. Shrill ideological appeals, he had found,
might be good devices for winning elections and gaining power,
but sober pragmatic approaches seemed necessary when wield-
ing power and running the government.

There are at least two dangers in the pragmatic method of
governance, however, and one of them proved to be Stephens's
undoing. The first is to become cynical, and the second is to become dull. By deemphasizing the moral content of his program
the politician risks ignoring it altogether and seeks power for
its own sake. His political career then becomes a ceaseless and
cynical exercise in determining and gratifying the public's will in
return for the public's votes. Political hacks and demagogues are
produced by this perversion of the pragmatic technique. Equally
great is the danger that by noting the complexities and ambigui-
ties in the political situation, the pragmatic politician fails to
take clear-cut moral positions on questions about which the
public is emotionally aroused; he thus appears to be "wishy-
washy" and indecisive in contrast to an ideological opponent
whose simplistic but clearly defined stands on such issues have
great voter appeal. The pragmatic power-holder, in short, is
often at the mercy of the ideological power-seeker in election
campaigns.

It was this latter pitfall that ended William D. Stephens's
political career. In the primary election of 1922 the conservative
wing of the Republican party went after Stephens's progressive
scalp.[4] They chose for their standard-bearer the incumbent state
treasurer, a pugnacious Quaker named Friend W. Richardson.
A flamboyant conservative whose bristling mustache and rotund

figure made him appear almost a caricature of the conservative, capitalistic "fat cat," Richardson made a clear-cut ideological appeal on the virtues of economy and limited government. He attacked Stephens and the Progressives as "spendthrift politicians" and promised to reduce his "extravagant" state budget by millions of dollars. Stephens complacently underestimated the appeal of the economy issue, which to him meant efficient management and not reduced expenditures, and he lost the election to Richardson by a narrow margin.[5] With this event the Progressive movement received its first great reverse.

The new governor wasted little time in trying to put his conservative ideas into practice. Ignoring the amenities in his inaugural address, the jowly executive attacked his predecessor, who was sitting nearby, for the "orgy of extravagance" which had allegedly characterized his administration, and he vowed to "put out of power the political machine which has dominated the State government." In February 1923 he submitted a biennial budget of several million dollars less than the previous one, much to the chagrin of the Progressives in the legislature who deplored the crippling cuts in education, social welfare, and many other state services. The Progressives had also lost control of the legislature as a result of the recent election, and the conservatives, led by Assembly Speaker and future Governor Frank Merriam, steered the Richardson budget through to passage. By vetoing a large number of bills on the grounds of their extravagance and by refusing adamantly to secure a new trial for Tom Mooney, Richardson further gladdened the hearts of conservatives and caused many to believe that the Progressive movement was dead at last.

Rumors of the demise of progressivism, however, turned out to be, like the reported death of Mark Twain, greatly exaggerated. Instead of rolling over and playing dead after the disastrous legislative session of 1923, the Progressives regrouped mainly around the leadership of Lieutenant Governor C. C. Young and organized the Progressive Voters' League (PVL). This group sprang immediately to the offensive, charging that Richardson's policies were delivering the state into the hands of big business and depriving the people of vital state services. The governor had reduced state funding for control of animal diseases, for example, as well as for fighting forest fires, and when a rash of fires broke out in the summer of 1923 as well as fortuitous epidemic of foot-and-mouth disease, the PVL charged him with responsibility for these disasters. The PVL demanded nothing less than a return of progressivism to power, and in the legislative elections of 1924 they picked up enough seats to secure a virtual standoff with the Richardson men and to force some concessions from them in the 1925 legislature. The biennial budget of that year was substantially larger than the previous one, especially in its appropriations for social welfare agencies, and the legislature ratified a national child labor amendment, making California one of only six states to do so during the decade. Both sides recognized, however, that these were only preliminary skirmishes before the big battle for the governorship in the coming election of 1926.

In this election the governor made a fatal though understandable mistake. A more prudent politician would probably have recognized that the progressive impulse was still vital in the state and that he should make some accommodation to it. Some shift in position from the ideological "right wing" of the political spectrum to the pragmatic and moderate "middle" would seem to be in order. The California electorate, despite its volatility, unpredictability, and occasional proneness to respond to sharp ideological appeals, has usually proven itself to be basically moderate, especially when times are normal, and the extremist incumbent usually finds it necessary to move toward the center in order to retain his office. Richardson, however, cast caution to the winds and mainly repeated his rhetoric of 1922. He condemned his opponents in the 1926 Republican primary as "radicals" and "socialists," and to prove himself the economizer par excellence he vetoed more than half of all the bills passed by the 1925 legislature! As a result his record as the greatest gubernatorial nay-sayer in California history is still unsurpassed.

His opponents, on the other hand, conducted a classic pragmatic Progressive campaign. The PVL chose Lieutenant Governor C. C. Young as its standard-bearer, and he not only called for a long list of typically Progressive programs—highway construction, water and hydroelectric development, forest preservation, tax revision, the completion of governmental reorganization, and the like—but went on to take two other significant positions on his opponent's pet theme of economy in government. For one thing he asserted that the subject was largely a pseudo-issue, because "economy" and Richardson's other favorite slogan, "law enforcement," were "so obviously the duty of any servant of the public that they can hardly be dignified with the title of issues." Secondly, he said that economy meant close supervision of the fiscal process and avoidance of waste rather than reduced expenditures, because, and here his language was remarkably candid, expanded budgets and increased expenditures were impossible to avoid while the state was undergoing its remarkably rapid growth during this decade.[6] Young was probably the first modern California politician to recognize a fundamental reality which has been the economizer's dilemma ever since: the larger the population, the greater the demands for governmental services and the larger the budgets. It might be thought that such an open admission that he intended to spend more of the people's money if elected would be a blueprint for political suicide, but such was not the case, for when the ballots were counted it was Governor Richardson who had gone down to defeat.[7]

    C. C. Young brought a modest renewal of the Progressive movement in California. A former school teacher and businessman and as colorless as weak tea, he had long been associated with the Republican progressives as a legislator, speaker of the assembly, and lieutenant governor; and as governor he became recognized as one of the most capable administrators ever to hold the office. He completed the process of governmental reorganization begun under Governor Stephens, revised the state statutes into a logical system of codes, and secured the passage of a number of humanitarian reforms. These included aid programs for the physically handicapped, needy, and blind, and the first modern comprehensive old-age pension law in the nation. In the fields of conservation and resource development he secured the establishment of pest-control stations at state borders, water conservation districts, and the basis of the state park system; at his urging the legislature authorized a survey of all the state's water resources and hydroelectric power sites and approved of public financing of both the Central Valley Project and the Boulder Canyon Project after having refused to endorse the latter during Richardson's administration.

Probably the best indication of Young's success as a progressive was his handling of fiscal and budgetary matters. An advocate of expanded state services and sound budgeting and cost-control techniques, he succeeded in increasing bank taxes to raise additional revenues, and, more importantly, he instituted a genuine comprehensive budget system with all state expenditured included so that for the first time the people could see what was being done with their taxes and how much was being spent. What they saw was, as Young had admitted, a heavy increase in public expenditures. The total biennial budget, which was under $100 million at the beginning of the decade, swelled to $194 million in the fiscal years 1927-1929, the first half of Young's term. In the next biennium (July 1, 1929, through June 30, 1931) Young and the legislature increased it to $244 million, and the state was on its way to the billion and multi-billion-dollar budgets of the modern era. While Young admitted that such budgets were "not drafted from the standpoint of economy alone," he did, like Stephens before him, emphasize that his accounting and disbursement procedures were in accordance with sound business practices. Even the large budget of 1929-1931 was, he asserted, "based upon an economy that will assure a businesslike, efficient, progressive and intelligent administration of the state's business." That Young could successfully present himself as businesslike and progressive at the same time was assured when he demonstrated that, despite these increased expenditures, the state had a $30 million treasury surplus by 1930. True to his progressive creed, he proposed that this surplus not be returned to the people in tax reductions, but retained for emergencies, spent partially on a building program in state institutions and partly for public works projects for victims of the Great Depression, which was beginning to be felt in the state.

With this rather remarkable record Young expected to be renominated in the Republican primary of 1930. His dream was shattered by two great stumbling blocks of the time, the depression and prohibition. The Great Depression proved devastating to incumbents all over the nation as they learned once again that if they expect the people to give them credit for good times they can also expect them to blame them for bad. Likewise prohibition, which rewarded many of its advocates, such as Young, with public office, could also prove to be a fickle benefactor. Although sentiment in favor of it was gradually changing, Young still zealously cultivated the "dry" vote in 1930. Unfortunately for him, so did one of his rivals, a conservative Los Angeles district attorney named Buron Fitts, and because the Anti-Saloon League waited too long before endorsing Young, the two "drys" divided the prohibitionist vote between them and enabled the "soaking wet" Mayor James Rolph of San Francisco to win the nomination and the governorship.

When Young passed from the political scene in January 1931, an era passed with him. The classic age of progressivism had now come to an end, and although many features of the Progressive movement would continue vital in the state's politics, its heyday of dominance was past, and the age of the New Deal was at hand.

CHAPTER TWO

Depression
Politics,
1931–1942

THE GREAT DEPRESSION caused more social trauma and upheaval in California than any event since the Gold Rush. Unlike the Gold Rush, however, whose negative aspects of cultural disruption and social disorder were counterbalanced by positive features of political development and economic growth, the depression had no positive attributes whatsoever. Instead, massive business failures, bankruptcies, losses of life savings, unemployment, lengthening relief lines (from 700,000 in 1930 to 1,250,000 in 1934), and a constant influx of penniless "Okies" and other refugees bedeviled the state. These disasters especially harassed the counties and local communities which were saddled with the responsibility of providing most of the unemployment relief and mainly from a source that was quickest to dry up in depression times—the property tax.

In this desperate situation Californians had two main options. They could resort to the conventional wisdom of *laissez faire,* reduce public expenditures, "tighten their belts," and wait for a "natural" upturn in economic conditions. Or they could adopt the "Keynesian" methods of the New Deal, greatly expanding governmental spending programs in relief and public employment and rely on private spending by relief recipients to stimulate demand for consumer goods and cause an upturn in employment. California, however, unlike the federal government, was constitutionally prohibited from engaging in large-scale deficit financing and deliberately unbalanced budgets. Consequently, increased spending had to be financed by increased taxation, and since it would be self-defeating to tax citizens who were already hard hit by the depression, those who advocated such policies proposed levying taxes that were "progressive" in character and would bear on those most able to pay. Progressive income taxes and severance taxes on oil extraction seemed fairest to the liberals and New Dealers who advocated such policies, while conservatives castigated all such proposals as "radical," "soak-the-rich," and "socialist" schemes. Since the stakes were high, the debate was bitter, and the California government, having to choose between these competing ideologies, was a storm center of controversy throughout the decade.

The first governor compelled to make such choices, and probably the least competent to do so, was James Rolph, Jr. Originally a Progressive, his nineteen years as mayor of San Francisco had remade him into a typical business-oriented Republican, and the ceremonial functions of his office had converted him from a political leader into a glad-handing official greeter who exuded irrepressible confidence and optimism. In his colorful campaign for governor in 1930 he all but ignored the depression and urged the voters instead to "smile with Sunny Jim." Even a year later he recommended that all Californians take a vacation to combat their depression blues, and acted on his own advice by going on a fishing trip.

The Great Depression, however, neither took a vacation nor allowed itself to be smiled away. The governor, a humane but weak man, did pity the depression's unfortunates and saw to it that most of the $30 million state treasury surplus was expended in their behalf, and he even anticipated the New Deal Civilian Conservation Corps by more than a year when he established a work camp program for unemployed young men. He also supported successfully the passage of the Central Valley Project Act of 1933, which authorized the construction of several large dams and canals on the Sacramento and San Joaquin rivers and the generation of cheap hydroelectric power, despite the strenuous opposition of various conservative forces, especially the

large power companies. When he came to the crucial question
of state budgets and taxation, however, the governor succumbed
entirely to the demands of the "reactionaries." Both his 1931-
1933 and his 1933-1935 budgets were very "tight" (the latter,
which called for $258 million, was $24 million less than the
previous biennial appropriations), and he endorsed the Riley-
Stewart tax initiative of 1933 which shifted some local tax
burdens to the state but financed the increased state outlays by a
highly regressive sales tax. When this measure passed, Rolph
vetoed an income tax measure also passed by the legislature on
the grounds that the sales tax made such a new tax unnecessary.
In his feverish urge to economize Rolph also proposed to raise
the eligibility age for state old-age pensions from 70 to 75 and
to shift the burden of the pension program back to the counties.
He further distinguished himself by attacking anyone advocat-
ing increased corporation taxes as "an enemy of the people,"
condoning mob violence against agricultural strikers in the Im-
perial Valley, and congratulating a lynch mob in San Jose for
hanging two kidnap-murder suspects. He embarrassed the conservatives who were probably relieved when he died suddenly
while campaigning for renomination in June 1934. His successor, Lieutenant Governor Frank Merriam, who captured the
Republican nomination against C. C. Young, seemed equally
conservative, however, when he used troops to end a longshoremen's strike in San Francisco. Thus it seemed to many that
the California Republicans had demonstrated a notorious political bankruptcy in dealing with the travails of the Great Depression.

Republican bankruptcy, of course, spelled Democratic opportunity. But before the California Democrats could capitalize
on their chances to gain control of the state government, they
had many obstacles to overcome. Plagued by internal divisions,
especially the North-South split now intensified by the prohibition issue, by inept leadership, by the crossfiling law which
benefited Republican incumbents, and by the state's refusal to
apportion legislative and congressional seats fairly (a decision
that cheated southern California and the cities of their due
representation), the Democrats had become a shadow party by
1930. With a voter registration disadvantage of three-to-one in
favor of the Republicans, they elected only a handful of legis-

lators during the 1920s (in one election the Democrats elected only three members to the eighty-seat assembly and in three different elections they failed to elect a single state senator), and only two congressmen. They also saw their gubernatorial candidate poll less than a third of the vote in 1922 and the national presidential candidate only 8.2 percent in 1924. Although the Democratic presidential candidate in 1928 made a more respectable showing, the party's gubernatorial aspirants in 1926 and 1930 did even worse than in 1922.

But in 1931 and 1932 the Democrats began getting the "breaks." The reapportionment act of 1931, which finally gave southern California its fair share of congressional and state assembly seats, also proved to be a boon for the party. Population increases brought about an increase in the state's congressional seats from 11 to 20, and 8 of those 9 new seats were awarded to the south. Moreover, whereas the Republicans in 1930 held 10 of the 11 seats, in the election of 1932 the Democrats gained 11 of the 20. In the assembly the south received 43 of the 80 seats, and in 1932 the Democrats increased their number in that body from 7 to 25 and established a trend which would lead to the party's capture of the house in 1936. The state senate, however, remained unapportioned in line with the notorious "Federal Plan" adopted in 1926, and as a result would remain a rural-dominated Republican stronghold until the 1960s.[1] Also, in 1932, for the first time since the passage of the national prohibition amendment, the "wets" (i.e., those in favor of repeal of prohibition) gained control of the legislature, repealed the state prohibition enforcement act, and put the state on record in favor of national repeal. When this was done by constitutional amendment in the following year, the divisive prohibition issue which had embittered and bedeviled the party for more than a decade passed from the scene.

Of course, the biggest Democratic gain was the Franklin D. Roosevelt landslide in the election of 1932 and the great popularity of the New Deal in succeeding years. This popularity caused party registration in the state to change from three-to-one in favor of the Republicans to three-to-two in 1932 and to a fifty-fifty split in 1934. (By 1936 it would become three-to-two in favor of the Democrats and has tended to remain fairly constant at that margin.) The state Democratic leadership strove to establish a sound working relationship with the national party organization and the Roosevelt administration, and to secure unity within its own ranks in order to gain the governorship and the legislature in 1934. The dominant figure in this effort was William G. McAdoo, a well-known Wilsonian Democrat who had moved to Los Angeles in 1922 and won the nomination for United States senator in 1932 against Justus Wardell, a long-time northern California Democratic leader who regarded McAdoo as an interloper and an upstart. McAdoo also won the state presidential primary that year as head of a slate of delegates to the Democratic national convention pledged to John N. Garner of Texas, while Wardell lost again as head of a slate committed to Franklin D. Roosevelt. When McAdoo dramatically delivered the California delegation to Roosevelt on the third ballot and went on to win a United States Senate seat in the same general election that brought Roosevelt into the White House, he was in a commanding position in Democratic party affairs in California.

He used his position ineptly. Again unwilling to support his rival, Justus Wardell, in his bid for the Democratic gubernatorial nomination in 1934, McAdoo persuaded an old associate from the Wilson administration, George Creel, to file for the nomination. Presenting themselves as moderates against the presumably conservative Wardell group and also against the allegedly "radical" Democrats represented by state senate candidate Culbert L. Olson, president of the Los Angeles Democratic Club, McAdoo and Creel attempted to play conventional politics in very unconventional times and in a very unconventional state. The miseries of the Great Depression had churned up many unorthodox characters and groups with many unorthodox political ideas, some of which were bound to appeal to California's unstable population. Already on the scene were the various self-help groups seeking to alleviate depression problems by bartering schemes, the Technocrats who sought to replace the monetary system with an energy system, the Utopian Society whose public psychodramas of social change called "cycles" afforded emotional if not economic relief to many, and especially the Townsend movement which was convinced that it could cure the depression through the payment of old-age pensions. The wise political leader would seek to attract at least some of these divergent groups and channel their political energies into constructive party purposes rather than dismiss them all as irresponsible crackpots (which many assuredly were), as McAdoo and Creel were wont to do. Since most of these groups had a much greater affinity for the Democrats and the New Deal than for the Republicans, the danger in ignoring them lay in the possibility that this would split the party and allow the Republicans to win.

The group that showed that this danger was real was the "Epic" movement led by Upton Sinclair. A widely read novelist and radical pamphleteer, Sinclair had twice run for governor on the Socialist ticket, but in 1933 he was persuaded to change his registration to Democratic and to draft a political program for the liberal wing of the party. Claiming that the platform he devised would "End Poverty in California," he abbreviated it to EPIC and henceforth it became known as the "Epic" program. Pygmalion-like, Sinclair fell in love with his handiwork and announced his candidacy for the governorship in order to implement it. Although opponents saw it as a grotesque monstrosity instead of a lovely work of art, the Epic platform was greeted with wild enthusiasm by hundreds of thousands of the depression-ravaged down-and-out. Although it contained several standard liberal features, such as tax reform bearing heavily on the wealthy and increased old-age pensions, the program's most controversial component was its "production for use" proposal. This scheme called on the state to make relief recipients self-supporting by placing some on idle land to grow food and others in idle factories to produce consumer items, the exchange of products to be facilitated by state-issued scrip money. A $300 million bond issue would finance the state acquisition of land and industrial plants. Although this hastily hatched scheme was hardly the sure-fire cure-all for the problems of the Great Depression that its fervent adherents claimed it to be, neither was it a conspiratorial blueprint for bolshevism as charged by its opponents. (Both the Socialist and Communist parties repudiated Sinclair's program as a sell-out to capitalism.)

Nevertheless, the party regulars, including both the Wardell and McAdoo-Creel factions, condemned Sinclair and his associates as crackpots and "reds." Since Sinclair's advocates included state senatorial candidate Culbert L. Olson, Sinclair's later campaign manager and future governor; Ellis Patterson, assembly candidate and future lieutenant governor; and Sheridan Downey, Sinclair's running mate for lieutenant governor and future United States senator, the party leaders were openly courting party fragmentation if Sinclair and his Epic followers won in the primary election.

And win they did. United in an organization called the End Poverty League, which sponsored thousands of local ad hoc organizations called Epic clubs, the Sinclair forces generated a pervasive and often hysterical mass enthusiasm for the program. Sinclair himself proved an adept campaigner, especially when he appeared on the same platform with his running mate, Sheridan Downey, who was a spellbinding orator. Although the press contemptuously referred to the two as "Uppie and Downey," they made an effective team. They proved it when they easily won their respective nominations along with Olson and Patterson and a number of other legislative candidates. Gleefully placing themselves in control of the party, they wrote the Epic program into the party platform at the state Democratic convention and confidently looked forward to leading a united Democratic party into battle against their Republican foes.

Instead they found themselves fighting a civil war with their own party brethren or encountering the passive resistance of slackers who refused to attack the enemy. Wardell defected first and was soon followed by Creel, who spuriously argued that Sinclair had revived his Epic program after the convention had rejected it! McAdoo silently sabotaged Sinclair's campaign by failing to support it, and he probably helped persuade President Roosevelt to avoid endorsing Epic after Sinclair had embarrassingly "gone out on a limb" by predicting that the president would support him. Thus it was the party regulars who abandoned the new leaders, repudiated their program, and provided the Republicans with much ammunition to fire at Sinclair and the Epic men.

The Republicans were quick to use it and to come up with additional charges of their own. Not content with merely repeating the oft-uttered allegations of Sinclair's radical and crackpot designs, they sifted through his voluminous writings to quote and misquote and to make many additional spectacular smears which were widely circulated in practically all of the state's newspapers. Not content with misrepresenting him as an atheist and practitioner of free love, they also charged that he was mentally defective and that the Epic slogan should read "Epileptic." With a fine disregard for consistency they also alleged that he was a sinister Communist conspirator who in reality had designed his slogan to mean "End Property, Introduce Communism." Furthermore, they charged that Sinclair was deliberately plotting to attract more hoboes, Okies, and "relief chiselers" into the state whose Epic motto would be "Easy Pickings in California." Some rare notes of humor were injected into the campaign by C. C. Young, who asserted that the Epic plan's unworkability would "End California in Poverty" rather than vice versa, and by third-party candidate Raymond Haight's campaign newspaper, the *EBIC Snooze,* which signified "Expose Bunk in California" and contrasted nicely with Sinclair's weekly newspaper, the *EPIC News.* Mainly, however, the Republican campaign was grimly serious, "a phobia lacking humor, fairness, and even a sense of reality," according to one observer, and waged by people who, "convinced that this is not politics but war . . . excuse their excesses on the ground that in war all's fair."[2]

There was, however, more to the Republican campaign than partisan excesses. Recognizing that the distresses of the masses were serious and that the party could not expect to gain their votes by relying merely on vituperation and the mouthing of right-wing clichés, the Republicans made many concessions to the obviously popular New Deal and sought to portray themselves as moderate, pragmatic reformers in contrast to the left-wing ideologues of the Epic movement. The party platform pointed with pride to the progressive tradition still represented by Hiram Johnson,[3] and called for more unemployment relief, supported collective bargaining for labor, endorsed the movement for a nationwide thirty-hour week and six-hour day, advocated enlarged old-age pensions, and recommended congressional consideration of the Townsend old-age pension plan. The latter was a particularly adroit, if cynical, move, since the plan was enormously popular, and since Sinclair foolishly, but honestly, had attacked the proposal because it sought to finance pensions from a highly regressive sales tax. Merriam, the Republican candidate for governor, not only enthusiastically endorsed all of these platform proposals and called a special session of the legislature to implement the relief measure, but also, unlike many others, refrained from gross personal attacks upon his opponent. Thereby he cultivated an image of himself as "the good, gray governor" (he was sixty-eight years old and more bald than gray), and the voice of reason and moderation opposing the foolishness and radicalism of Epic.

Whatever the "merits" of the Republican campaign tactics, they worked, and Governor Frank Merriam was easily elected in his own right. Merriam is usually written off as a "reactionary" by most historians (mainly because he used the National Guard against striking longshoremen in San Francisco in 1934 and state highway patrolmen against Salinas lettuce strikers in 1936) or as a do-nothing conservative who caused California to "mark time" in its struggle against the Great Depression while the rest of the nation was marching forward under the glorious banner of the New Deal. However, it is necessary to distinguish between Merriam's conservative rhetoric and his moderate-to-liberal actions, and if this is done he can be viewed as the governor who brought the New Deal to California, hesitatingly perhaps, on tiptoe, and a little shamefacedly, but he brought it nevertheless. An experienced politican from Long Beach (since 1916 he had served as assemblyman and speaker, state senator, lieutenant governor, Governor Richardson's campaign manager, and chairman of the Republican State Central Committee), he knew that the people wanted more from their government than the conservatives in his party were prepared to give, and his administration was a four-year balancing act in which he attempted to implement as many New Deal–type policies as possible without provoking a revolt from his original backers. Pragmatic conservatism perhaps best describes his political performance.

Calling in his inaugural address for a program of "social justice without socialism," Merriam proposed and secured the establishment of a State Emergency Relief Administration (SERA, later SRA) which made the state eligible to receive funds from the federal government for unemployment relief under the many grant-in-aid programs that were a hallmark of the New Deal. For the same purpose he backed the passage of the Hornblower Act of 1935 which liberalized the state old-age pension law, enabling California to receive additional funds under the Social Security Act passed the same year. This and other social legislation caused the state budget to swell to $400 million in 1935 and to almost $450 million two years later. New expenditures called for new taxes, and during his first biennium Merriam unabashedly sought and secured the passage of a state income tax and increased levies on banks, corporations, inheritances, and retail sales. The sales tax law of 1935, moreover, was also a liberalized measure (pushed through the legislature by Senator Olson and his fellow "Epics") because it exempted from taxes groceries, fuel, and prescription drugs. In his second biennium he swung back to a more fiscally conservative position by pointing pridefully to a $21 million treasury surplus and invoking a slogan of "no new taxes" against the Epic "spenders" who wished to proceed much further and faster with social legislation.

By this time Merriam was beginning to encounter the perils of moderation in immoderate times and in an abnormal state. His record of modest achievement would probably have ensured his reelection in a more prosperous era and in a less volatile state where control of the party apparatus meant more than personal popularity and rapport with powerful interest groups. But in Hollywood-oriented, depression-ridden California he was scorned by many as dull, conservative, and colorless, and when he called for increased taxes on liquor and severance taxes on oil and other minerals, he aroused the animosity of two of the most powerful business interests in the state. Even worse, he antagonized their legislative representative, one of the most flamboyant and capable lobbyists ever to "grace" a legislative chamber, Arthur Samish.

"Artie" Samish could only have happened in California. When the Johnson progressives deliberately weakened political parties in the interest of encouraging nonpartisanship, they created a situation where candidates must look elsewhere for encouragement, direction, and support. Where else but to the public at large and the media if they were colorful enough to attract attention, and to special-interest groups which would finance their campaigns? Of course, such groups extracted a price for their support, namely legislative backing on issues that concerned them. The legislature thus became a vast "com-

modity market," in the words of one analyst,[4] whereby legislators, who were often paid consultants and legal representatives
of the special interests that paid their campaign costs, voted for
or against legislation that their patrons supported or opposed. It
was probably inevitable that some super lobbyist would emerge
from this situation who would represent a large number of
powerful special-interest groups and thus become a backroom
czar of the legislative process. This is what Samish did, and by
the mid-1930s he had become, as he later characterized himself,
"governor of the legislature."

Not surprisingly Samish was incensed when "the other governor," Merriam, turned against two of his largest clients, the
liquor and mining industries. Samish was especially angered
since he had originally supported Merriam for governor. Calling
him a "bald-headed son of a bitch" and a "dirty old bastard,"
Samish allegedly said, "I helped you get into that governor's
chair. And I'll get your ass out of it too."[5] His method of de-
thronement was to encourage and support Lieutenant Governor
George Hatfield to run against Merriam in the gubernatorial
primary of 1938. Hatfield was much more conservative than
Merriam and had the backing of many right-wing groups, such
as the notorious Associated Farmers, which resented Merriam's
alleged "sell-out" to the New Deal. The resourceful governor
responded, however, with a counterattack of his own. A grand
jury inquiry was already under way in Sacramento investigating
charges of bribery of state legislators by lobbying groups, and
Merriam secured a legislative appropriation of $50,000 to assist
the investigation. The grand jury report and a subsequent report by Howard Philbrick, an investigator for the district attorney's office, were extremely critical of various legislators and
lobbyists, including Samish and Hatfield when the latter had
been a state legislator. The discrediting of Hatfield probably
contributed to Merriam's renomination in the primary, but the
lingering rancor and divisiveness within the Republican party
jeopardized his chances for reelection in the fall of 1938.

While the Republicans were rending their party fabric by
internecine strife, the Democrats were finally gaining a short-
lived unity. Although there were several prominent Democratic
candidates in the 1938 gubernatorial primary, state senator Culbert L. Olson had attracted the most publicity. He easily won

the nomination with the slogan "Bring the New Deal to California." Although much of the New Deal was already there, Olson argued for enactment of additional liberal legislation, such as increased welfare payments and enlarged old-age pensions, the upgrading and reform of state institutions, tax reform based entirely on ability to pay, public ownership of public utilities, and government sale of electric power to the consumer from the Central Valley Project. Olson campaigned for these and other policies with a crusader's zeal and once again showed that the ideological approach to politics is an effective way to win elections so long as the opponent is perceived by the public as familiar and dull. Olson won decisively and ended California's forty-year drouth for Democratic governors.

The liberal Olson was an unusual governor in many respects. He took his campaign rhetoric too seriously and attempted to administer the office with the same ideological zeal with which he had won it. Apparently oblivious to the fact that the national New Deal was over when he took office in January 1939, that the Democrats controlled only one house of the state legislature (the assembly), and that many of the Democrats in both houses were conservatives or mavericks or both, Olson dumped a detailed reform program into the legislature's lap and provided almost no leadership to get the program enacted. In part he was a victim of circumstances, for he suffered two personal misfortunes in the crucial early weeks of the 1939 legislative session. His health unexpectedly failed him, and after being confined to bed for several weeks, he suffered a further shock when his wife died suddenly. Also, one of his first official acts was to pardon Thomas Mooney, the labor martyr who had languished in prison for twenty-two years, probably undeservedly. A courageous act of simple justice and probably Olson's greatest claim to fame, the pardon nevertheless infuriated many conservatives and cast an aura of "radicalism" around the governor which he was never able to dissipate. The aura was in fact enhanced when he showed sympathy for California's most abused proletarians, the agricultural workers, by attempting to enforce laws requiring decent housing for them and by encouraging the U.S. Senate's La Follette Committee investigations of deprivations of civil liberties in the state. This committee made damaging revelations about the growers' mistreatment of farm laborers and was casti-

gated by the Associated Farmers and other grower organizations as being sympathetic to communism, an allegation that was
also made against Olson.

In this situation it is not surprising that Olson's first legislative
session was a resounding failure. A shifting conservative coalition defeated or stifled in committee every one of his proposed
reforms, reduced his proposed budget by tens of millions of
dollars, cut relief funds out of the main budget bill, and began
the procedure of doling out minimal relief appropriations to
cover only a short period. This destroyed Olson's effort to
reform the State Relief Administration (SRA) somewhat along
the lines of Epic's old "production for use" proposal and necessitated frequent special sessions of the legislature to pass new
interim relief appropriations. In this debacle of 1939 the governor could take pride in only two things, the Mooney pardon and
the defeat of a weird movement known as "Ham and Eggs."

"Ham and Eggs," also known as the Retirement Life Payments Association and "Thirty Dollars Every Thursday," was
another of those California happenings that probably could
have transpired nowhere else. Like the Townsend movement it
was an aged-welfare scheme, but unlike that movement whose
founder was probably sincere but deluded, Ham and Eggs was
dominated by leaders (first Robert Noble and then the brothers
Willis and Lawrence Allen) who resembled money-making
racketeers more than serious social leaders. The scheme proposed to pay pensions of $30 a week to all unemployed persons
over age fifty, but the payments were to be made not in money
but in California "scrip" which it was hoped would circulate like
money. Because of a requirement that the scrip be stamped
every week its costs purportedly would be self-liquidating. Although the plan's weaknesses were self-evident to many, it soon
became incredibly popular when it burst onto the political scene
as an initiative constitutional amendment during the primary
election campaign of 1938. All politicians had to come to grips
with it, and Olson somewhat reluctantly gave it a qualified endorsement while his fellow liberals, Ellis Patterson running for
lieutenant governor and Sheridan Downey campaigning for the
U.S. Senate, enthusiastically praised it. All three won; Downey's
victory retired William G. McAdoo to private life despite President Roosevelt's endorsement and warnings against those who

promised "short-cuts to utopia and fantastic financial schemes." Although the Ham and Eggs measure failed to pass, its proponents succeeded in placing an even more sweeping measure on the ballot in 1939, and they badgered Olson incessantly to call a special election for the proposal in midsummer when Ham and Eggs enthusiasm would be at its height. Olson, however, foiled the plan's backers when he set the election for November, giving the opposition time to mount a counterattack against it, an opposition that Olson himself now joined. As a result the measure lost in the election, and even many conservatives praised the governor for his part in scotching the aberrant crusade.

Any possibility for a reconciliation between Olson and conservative forces soon faded, however. In the special session of the legislature of 1940, necessitated by the calculated shortage of relief funds, Olson angered the opposition by loading the legislative call with additional proposals, including several that had been defeated the previous year. At this point a coalition of Republicans and conservative Democrats launched a devastating counterattack. The Republicans had already deprived Lieutenant Governor Ellis Patterson of any voice in the selection of state senate committees, and now this coalition united in the assembly to unseat as speaker the Olsonite Paul Peek and elect in his stead Gordon Garland, a militantly anti-Olson Democrat. Garland's first official act was to rip out the telephone that reportedly linked the speaker's desk with the governor's office and to declare his intention to reverse "the increasing trend toward collectivism." The legislature then proceeded to defeat all of the governor's "extra" legislative proposals and not only reduced his relief request radically, despite the fact that unemployment was rising rapidly at the time, but launched a full-scale investigation into the State Relief Administration, charging that it was riddled with Communists. Surprisingly, two assemblymen making the most sensational charges of this sort were Jack Tenney and Samuel Yorty, both from Los Angeles and heretofore considered slightly to the left of the administration but now about to enter upon prolonged and stormy careers as red-baiters. Anticipating Watergate by thirty years, the inept governor was further humiliated when some personal employees of his were caught "bugging" Speaker Garland's hotel room with a dictograph.[6] The governor's wounded reputation never recovered from the debacle of 1940.

Although Governor Olson successfully campaigned to head a Democratic ticket pledged to President Roosevelt's renomination in the summer of 1940, his association with the national administration did little to restore his political credibility. (This despite the fact that California gave FDR large majorities in all four of his elections.) The approach and outbreak of World War II and its attendant prosperity made his program irrelevant, and when the popular Republican attorney general Earl Warren announced his candidacy for the governorship, Olson's political days were numbered. But he compiled a record of indistinction on one other issue before he passed from the scene. This was the wartime internment of the resident Japanese. The "relocation" of that hapless minority by the FDR government was supported nearly unanimously by the state's population, which was aroused by the attack on Pearl Harbor. Most politicians, liberal and conservative alike, reflected the popular anxiety, and Olson was no exception. Even so, in this questionable course he was outdone by Earl Warren, who earnestly backed the mass incarceration in the early months of 1942 and may have reaped political advantage from it. At any rate he demonstrated his popularity when he crossfiled and almost defeated Olson on the Democratic ticket as he won handily on his own. Warren's election as governor in November 1942 surprised no one, and Olson gracefully retired to private life famous in the annals of California politics for what he failed to achieve.

CHAPTER THREE

War, Warren, and Knight, 1943–1958

EARL WARREN was the most significant and commanding personage in mid-century California politics. Often compared with Hiram Johnson, he did admire and resemble him politically, although personally they were very different. While Johnson was grim, insecure, and abrasively demanding in his personal relationships, Warren in his private life was the same genial, straightforward, sincere family man that he persuasively professed to be in his public appearances. No politician, with the possible exception of Dwight Eisenhower, exploited the "nice guy" image more successfully, and perhaps no other deserved to. Growing greatly in political stature after his election to the governorship in 1942, he was returned to office by an enthusiastic electorate in the primary election of 1946. By crossfiling successfully on the Democratic ticket against the hapless attorney general, Robert Kenny, Warren became the only governor in history to be elected on both major party tickets in the fall election. In 1950 he set another record as the only governor in California history to be elected to a third term when he overwhelmed Democratic candidate James Roosevelt (a son of FDR) by more than a million votes. By this time he had become a national political figure, having declined the Republican vice presidential nomination in 1944 and accepted it in 1948, and he made an unsuccessful bid for the presidential nomination against Eisenhower in 1952. When he began an even more distinguished career as Chief Justice of the United States in 1953, he left behind him a political void which no subsequent California public figure has been entirely able to fill.

It is one thing to gain office, and quite another to achieve anything with it. It is Warren's record of political achievement that is his greatest measure of stature and historical significance. In an era of war, postwar upheaval, and unprecedented economic and population growth, an era that in many ways is still with us, he is customarily credited with devising policies that not only enabled the state to cope with these changes but also enabled it to become the locale of one of the most advanced societies of modern times. An acute recognition of the pervasive power of growth and a pragmatic willingness to use the power of the state to deal with it are perhaps the main keys to understanding Warren's political performance. Although his pragmatic nonpartisanship and his commitment to governmental activism often aroused the right-wing ideologues in his party to condemn him as a "radical" or a "socialist" or worse, historians tend to classify him as a political moderate more successful than most at protecting individual rights, preserving basic institutions, and promoting needed changes without being overwhelmed by them. If Governor Frank Merriam was a pragmatic conservative, Warren can be classed as a pragmatic liberal whose political activism was tempered by his avoidance of ideological excess and whose enormous popularity kept California politics on an even keel in an otherwise turbulent era.

There were two elements in Warren's background that make a mockery out of the charges of his "radicalism." One was his life-long Republicanism and the other was his long career in law enforcement. Except for very brief stints as a lawyer in private practice, a soldier in World War I, and as a legislative aide, his entire pregubernatorial career was mainly that of a prosecuting attorney. As a deputy district attorney and district attorney of Alameda County during the 1920s and 1930s, he became widely known as a formidable enemy of organized crime, and was elected president of the State Association of District Attorneys in recognition of his effectiveness. Similarly, his anti-crime crusade as state attorney general (1939–1942) and his proven administrative capability in reorganizing that office brought him national attention as president of the National Association of Attorneys General in 1940. While some of his later U.S. Supreme Court decisions have made it fashionable to criticize him for being "soft on crime," there were felons and ex-felons about the state who, having experienced first-hand his prosecutorial zeal, regarded this allegation of softness with wry skepticism.

Equally spurious was the charge that Warren was not a "real Republican" because of his liberalism. The facts were, of course, that the Republican party had been split between its conservative and liberal (or progressive) wings since the progressive upsurge in 1910, and Warren attached himself to the latter in the same year and remained with that faction of the party throughout his career. Furthermore, he played an active role in party affairs, serving as delegate to national conventions as early as 1928, and as chairman of the Republican State Central Committee in the crucial years 1935–1936. His service in the latter capacity was vital, for here he played a major role in saving the party from the twin dangers that threatened to destroy it— unwieldy organization and the voter registration revolution which brought a mass shift in party allegiance from predominantly Republican to heavily Democratic during the 1930s. The unwieldiness of political party organization had been deliberately contrived by the progressives a generation earlier so as purposely to weaken parties, which they identified with corruption and entrenched special interests, and to strengthen voter independence and nonpartisanship, which they equated with civic virtue and the public interest. As a result the state central committees became huge organizations dominated by candidates and officeholders and precluded from effective decision-making and party coordination on account of their size. The county central committees and the state executive committees, on the other hand, were legally precluded from effective leadership by being prohibited from nominating and endorsing candidates in the primary elections. Republicans found it easy to live with this anarchic system so long as it hurt the Democrats more than it did them, but when California Republicans began to defect in droves to the Democrats it was up to Warren and the Republican leadership to find a solution to the problem.

The answer to their prayers came with the founding of the California Republican Assembly (CRA) in 1934. Beginning as a voluntary liberal Republican club movement after the nation-wide party losses in the 1932 elections, the organization was consolidated under a statewide charter by Warren and his close associate Edward Shattuck to coordinate GOP affairs under less conservative leadership. Being a "private" organization, it was not bound by the legal prohibition against preprimary endorse-ments, and as it grew in numbers and influence many of the regular party officers joined it and found it a convenient vehicle from which to coordinate party affairs and maximize the party's effectiveness at the polls at the very time that its popular base was eroding by shrinking voter registration. Although some-times condemned, and with some justice, as Earl Warren's political machine, the CRA must be given credit for the remark-able performance of the Republican party in dominating the entire state government of California (except for the brief and ineffectual Olson administration) for twenty-five years after the Democrats became the majority party in the state. Although other factors contributed to the Republican achievement—incumbency, crossfiling, gerrymandering, widespread news-paper support—the superior party organization under CRA leadership was a significant factor, and Warren's role in bringing this about shows him to be a loyal and effective Republican.

If Warren was a certified Republican, then what kind of party man was he? Three adjectives come immediately to mind in answering this question. He was pragmatic; he was "nonparti-san"; he was progressive. Warren's pragmatism (his own favorite word in describing his political actions in his memoirs) consisted primarily of avoiding ideological slogans when devising public policies and, instead, deriving policies from detailed empirical studies of actual social situations. Armed with an array of facts and statistics provided by such studies, he would proceed to propose policies largely unaffected by ideological preconcep-tions. The conduct of the studies themselves was shrewdly cal-culated to engender grass-roots support, since they were often made by citizens' advisory groups and special commissions which could be counted on to publicize their findings and popularize their proposed solutions. Warren himself was acutely aware of the all-important role of publicity and public relations in modern California politics, and he ceaselessly used both the newspaper and the radio to engender and maintain popular support for his policies. The biweekly press conference and the monthly "Report to the People" over the airwaves were devices that the popular governor employed to squeeze an often reluctant legislature into disgorging the legislation he wanted.

Warren's relations with the legislature were also highly pragmatic. Unlike Olson he recognized its political independence and its constitutional equality with the executive. Consequently he did not "lobby" it excessively on behalf of his pet legislation, nor did he attempt to get his supporters into key positions within it. In 1947 he accepted uncomplainingly the assembly's election as speaker Orange County's Sam Collins, whose "political philosophy," according to one authority, "paralleled that of Calvin Coolidge." On the other hand, in the words of another observer, "he always had the legislature over a barrel. Each time they met, Warren was either a candidate for Governor or for President. They couldn't áfford to fight him."[1] Often the legislature had the upper hand, however, and Warren frequently chose to compromise with the legislature rather than fight it head-on. The interaction resulted in the amazing success of nintey percent of his legislative proposals which became law in one form or another, a remarkable achievement for any executive.

Warren's "nonpartisanship" was a more controversial aspect of his career. In one respect it carried a note of fallaciousness, since Warren was a life-long, card-carrying Republican. But like the Johnson progressives of an earlier era and partly for the same reasons, he wore the party label loosely in public and encouraged the electorate to "vote the man, not the party." This cliché also served as a handy justification for the expediential crossfiling practice, which might not otherwise withstand a close moral scrutiny. But crossfiling, which was a convenient luxury for Johnson's generation to attract Democrats into an already dominant Republican majority, had become an absolute necessity for Warren-era Republicans who had to woo Democrats into a minority Republican party in order to stay in office. Not surprisingly Warren studiously avoided emphasizing his Republicanism before a largely Democratic electorate. Instead he presented himself as "governor of all the people," and he steadfastly refused to endorse other Republican candidates for statewide office or to merge his campaign with theirs. Although this tactic earned him the enmity of Republican ideologues, it worked brilliantly for the party as well as himself. With less than forty percent of the registered voters, the party regained control of the governorship and the legislature in 1942 and held it for sixteen years. Furthermore, the Republicans continued to dominate the state's congressional delegation, and throughout Warren's tenure, the Democrats gained part-time control of only one state office, the attorney generalship. In the light of such a record, the term "Warren magic" takes on more meaning than much other journalistic hyperbole.

Even more important than Warren's pragmatism was his progressivism, for this relates directly to what he did with political power rather than to how he attained and retained it. What he did was to advance the progressive tradition of governmental activism in dealing with perceived public needs in a time of great social growth and change. Like the avowed progressive governors Stephens and Young before him, he believed that a rapidly growing society needed expanded governmental services and that this in turn required increased tax revenues and expanded budgets. The annual state budget grew from $394,-745,000 to $1,271,447,000 during his decade in office, and Warren's legislative messages were replete with requests for funds to deal with the needs of the present and to prepare for the demands of the future. In 1945 he secured authorization for the establishment of several special construction projects to serve as "shock absorbers" for the anticipated economic disruption and mass unemployment induced by the slowing of defense production after World War II. This policy continued for several years and is credited not only with rejuvenating the state's rundown buildings and institutional facilities but also with easing California's transition to a peacetime economy. Later messages noted the problems created by the great population growth during and after the war and the necessity of planning for and funding the increased needs in state services (schools and highways being only the most obvious) caused by such growth. The Korean War induced him to call for more funds for veterans' benefits and the establishment of a postwar planning and reemployment policy, and he consistently sought to fund such projects out of current revenues much more than by bond issues.

Like Governor Young in the 1920s Warren sought to protect himself against charges of fiscal irresponsibility by sound budget practices and by the avoidance of large revenue surpluses. In 1944, for example, when wartime prosperity brought sharp increases in tax receipts, he pushed through a bill to reduce income, sales, bank, and corporation tax rates, but retained a considerable portion of the surplus as a "rainy day fund" to finance some of the aforementioned construction projects. On the other hand, when he thought a tax increase was warranted, such as his demand for increased gas taxes to finance his highway construction program in 1947, he showed himself willing to engage (and defeat) in political battle the most powerful special interest in the state, the oil lobby.

More controversial were Warren's battles royal with two other powerful interests, the electric power companies and the California Medical Association. The former dispute involved Warren's support of the proposal to allow the federal government to construct transmission lines from its electric power generating plants in the Central Valley Project and sell power to publicly owned utility districts rather than sell its power to private power companies (especially the Pacific Gas and Electric Company) which would then retail it to the consumer. Proponents of the scheme castigated their opponents as "monopolists," while opponents branded their antagonists as "socialists." Many conservative Republicans regarded Warren as a socialist or worse because of his support of the plan. In the latter years of Warren's administration, the issue was resolved by compromise with the private power companies probably gaining most from the settlement.

In his struggle with the California Medical Association (CMA), Warren went down to a definitive if "heroic" defeat. In 1945 he proposed the establishment of a comprehensive health insurance system financed, like Social Security, by employer and employee contributions of one and one-half percent each. Although he had sounded out the president and executive committee of the CMA on the plan in advance and had received no objection from them, the CMA launched an immediate attack upon the proposal, branding it with the dread words "socialized medicine." So effective was the mass propaganda effort that when the measure was killed in legislative committee, one legislator averred that the lawmakers were not voting against Warren but against Stalin. Warren, refusing to acknowledge that his scheme had been hatched in the Kremlin (other opponents had branded it as nazism), resubmitted it to the legislature three additional times in subsequent years. The CMA, however, employing the famous professional campaign firm of Whitaker and Baxter (ironically, the same company that had handled Warren's original campaign for governor), defeated it every time. In fact Whitaker and Baxter, capitalizing on this success, went on to a greater "triumph" when they were employed to defeat President Harry Truman's national health insurance plan during the same years.

Although frustrated in this instance, Warren secured other advances in the public health field. Most satisfying personally was the passage of a law providing medical and hospitalization payments for sick and disabled workers under the state's unemployment compensation system. Here the governor outmaneuvered the CMA by showing that the same organization had originally favored this as an alternative to his health insurance plan but was now hypocritically opposed to it. Also of great significance was the vast upgrading and modernization of the state Public Health Service, which oversaw the construction of many new county hospitals, and the establishment in 1945 of the State Department of Mental Hygiene, which was designed, in Warren's words, to "take California out of the asylum age and put her into the hospital age." The department actually did more than that, since it not only supervised the construction and staffing of several modern mental hospitals, but also inaugurated the modern system of outpatient clinics for the treatment of many less seriously disturbed patients in their own neighborhoods. Warren also secured substantial increases in the state's Aid to the Blind program, but his efforts to do the same for the Aid to the Disabled program were frustrated by economizing Republicans until the administration of his successor, Goodwin Knight.

True to his progressive sentiments Warren also secured substantial increases in old-age pensions and in welfare payments under the Aid to Families with Dependent Children program. And in line with the same outlook he often proposed enactments to benefit the wage laborer. The son of a railroad worker and a "self-made man," he knew the devastating personal consequences of joblessness and sought unsuccessfully to establish a full employment commission to minimize postwar unemployment. He did secure considerable increases in unemployment insurance payments and the aforementioned grants to the medically unemployed, and when he opposed various antiunion measures— antipicketing, antifeatherbedding, and "right-to-work" bills— he secured the endorsement of the State Federation of Labor in his bid for reelection in 1946.[2] He forfeited that endorsement in 1950, however, after he failed to veto a "hot cargo" bill, came out in opposition to jurisdictional strikes, and opposed a labor-backed initiative to apportion the state senate more fairly.[3] The rank-and-file laboring men seemingly continued to support him, however, as he ran well in working-class districts. They were probably right to regard Warren as labor's friend and in some respects in advance of his times, as when he fought unsuccessfully to have farm laborers included within the unemployment insurance and worker's compensation systems, for example, and when he sought to broaden the worker's compensation system itself.

Equally advanced was the governor's position on the Negro in American society. Acutely aware that the severest form of racial discrimination against blacks was in the area of employment, he called for a fair employment practices statute in 1945 and for a state commission to enforce nondiscrimination laws against employers and labor unions alike in 1946. When the bills failed in the legislature, as did an initiative in 1946, Warren continued to press for such legislation throughout the remainder of his administration. Although his efforts failed, any close student of Warren's career need not have been surprised when Chief Justice Warren later wrote and delivered the landmark desegregation decision of 1954 which helped inaugurate the modern civil rights revolution still under way. In one of the strange vagaries of human nature, however, while he was exhibiting his enlightenment regarding the black in America, he seems to have remained ambiguous on the Japanese question for an indefinite period of time. He continued to defend Japanese incarceration during the war, calling it "one of the things that saved our state from terrible disorders and sabotage" despite the fact that no sabotage had occurred and that there was no evidence that the Japanese intended to commit any. When some suggested that "loyal" Japanese be allowed to return to the state to relieve the farm labor shortage, Warren declared that such a policy would be "a body blow to our security."[4] On the other hand, when selected Japanese internees were allowed to return to California over the shrill objections of many of the state's "patriots," Warren took strong action to protect the rights of those returning, especially against the revived Ku Klux Klan and other local mobsters. Not until he penned his posthumously published memoirs in the early 1970s did he specifically repudiate his actions in behalf of Japanese incarceration.

On other political matters he again took rather advanced stands. He backed the passage of more stringent lobby control acts in 1949 and 1950 mainly to deal with "Artie" Samish, whose arrogance had earned the state embarrassing national publicity. But it was the federal government that ultimately ended Samish's career a few years later by sending him to prison for income tax evasion.

Much more controversial was the governor's stance on the "subversion" issue. Although (fortunately) the feeling of these years is difficult to recapture today, in the early Cold War era most Americans were convinced that the great danger to the country came not only from Soviet Communism in the international arena but from Communists, traitors, spies, "reds," "pinks," "subversives," "fellow travelers," and "dupes" within the nation itself. Many politicians proved more than willing to exploit such fears, especially by using congressional and state legislative committees and other investigating agencies to inquire into the personal lives, political beliefs, and past associations of thousands of individuals suspected of "disloyalty." When such victims could not prove that they were not "disloyal" (proving a negative is logically impossible) or refused to cooperate with their interrogators when asked to give names of former associates or by taking the Fifth Amendment, they were smeared as subversives and subjected to many injustices by a hostile public. On the national scene these tactics came to be known as "McCarthyism" after their most notorious practitioner, Senator Joseph McCarthy of Wisconsin. California's "McCarthy" was state senator Jack Tenney, chairman of the legislature's Un-American Activities Committee which conducted the same type of "witch hunts" on the state level. Other political figures became involved in such activities, probably the best known being Richard Nixon, whose 1946 campaign for Congress against Jerry Voorhis and his 1950 senatorial campaign against Helen Gahagan Douglas were rife with charges questioning the loyalty of both opponents, charges that Nixon himself later regretted, saying they were made when he was a very young man.[5]

Two California institutions that also suffered from the anti-Communist hysteria were the movie industry and the University of California. The attack on moviemakers and performers for allegedly propagandizing Americans on behalf of left-wing causes was primarily done at the national and congressional levels and needs no extended treatment here, but the assault on the university was a home-grown product. Pressured by the Tenney committee, the university Board of Regents voted to require all professors and university employees to take a sweeping loyalty oath in addition to the oath already required by state employees. When some refused they were dismissed, and then the highly publicized and emotional controversy was carried into the courts. While opponents contended that the basic issues were those of civil rights and academic freedom, oath proponents asserted that "flags would fly in the Kremlin" if the oath were rejected and that it would be necessary to organize squads of "twentieth-century vigilantes" to put down the Communist uprisings that would take place in the state.

While such assertions can be dismissed as the vaporings of either the politically hysterical or the politically dishonest, they should not obscure the fact that there was a genuine far-left movement in the state about which many moderates were sincerely worried. Henry A. Wallace's candidacy for the presidency in 1948 on the Independent Progressive party ticket was dominated, or at least strongly influenced, by the Communist party but nevertheless was backed by many liberal Democrats and Hollywood celebrities.[6] In 1950 Bernadette Doyle, an avowed member of the Communist party, polled more than 600,000 votes for the nonpartisan office of state superintendent of public instruction, although her party affiliation was probably unknown to many of those who voted for her. The danger of the far-left movement, if there was one, was probably not its numerical strength, which was apparently much smaller than that of the far right, but that, like the far right, it would help polarize the electorate into two deadly antagonistic extremist camps with the voice of moderation becoming that of a dwindling and muffled minority. Democracy itself could have become a casualty of such a confrontation.

More than any other single individual, Earl Warren probably helped to save the state from such a political fate. With his enormous popularity he isolated both political extremes and staked out a broad path in political middle of the road down which the vast majority of California citizens followed. Although a committed anti-Communist, he abjured efforts to smear non–Communist party members with vague allegations of Communist associations or sympathies.[7] As early as 1944 he eliminated from a "canned" speech given him by the Republican presidential campaign committee references to "the Earl Browder–Sidney Hillman Communist allied Political Action Committee" which was purportedly supporting President Roosevelt's reelection. This contrasts graphically with Richard Nixon's campaign rhetoric against Voorhis two years later which bristled with attacks on the "Communist dominated" Political Action Committee allegedly backing Voorhis. In 1948, when fellow Republicans were charging that subversives had crept into California government as well as into the movie industry, Warren pooh-poohed the charges, refused to institute a loyalty check on state employees, and pledged himself to protect Hollywood from being smeared by irresponsible charges. And in 1949–1950 he played a major role in defusing the explosive oath controversy at the University of California. Arguing that the oath would be ineffectual since committed Communists "would take the oath and laugh," he also asserted that it was unconstitutional since the Regents did not possess the power to require an oath in addition to the one in the state constitution, which was already required of all state employees. This reasoning proved correct, or at least partially so, as the state supreme court invalidated the oath and ordered the nonsigning professors reinstated in 1951, but the court did not invalidate the loyalty oath that the legislature, as opposed to the Regents, had enacted as the Levering Act in 1950. Warren disliked this act, especially since it had been drafted by one of his right-wing Republican foes, Assemblyman Harold Levering of Los Angeles, and he ultimately "got even" when as U.S. Chief Justice he led in the rendering of a number of antioath decisions which eventually helped prompt the California supreme court to invalidate the Levering Act in 1967.

By 1952 Warren had alienated many Republicans in the conservative wing of the party. Led by Congressman Thomas Werdel of Bakersfield, the right wing sought to embarrass him in his bid for the presidency that year by placing a Werdel slate in the presidential primary in opposition to his. When the voters chose Warren by a two-to-one majority and, in the general election, turned Werdel out of his seat in the House of Representatives, it seemed to most that as long as Warren was at the helm, moderate activism rather than extremism would characterize the mainstream of California politics. When Warren left the political arena, as he did the following year, it surprised no one that a virulent power struggle began to take place for a dominant position in the Republican party.

The party in California was by no means bereft of leadership when Warren departed in 1953 to become Chief Justice of the United States. In fact it was plagued by too many "big guns" vying for supremacy. In the vice presidency sat Richard Nixon, a "heart beat away from the presidency," and Eisenhower's presidential heart beat very unsteadily. In the U.S. Senate California's popular senior senator William F. Knowland gained national prominence as majority leader in that august body, and later as minority leader when the Democrats regained control of Congress in 1954. The junior senator, Thomas Kuchel, appointed to succeed Nixon in 1952 when the latter moved into the vice presidency, was elected for the remainder of the term in 1954 and reelected for a full term in 1956, and was obviously a "comer" in California politics. And, last but not least, there was Goodwin J. Knight in the governor's chair.

Knight was an old hand in California politics. A lawyer and businessman (he owned a gold mine in Kern County), he was a life-long Republican who began as a Hiram Johnson progressive and had turned conservative by the 1930s. His efforts on behalf of Frank Merriam in 1934 were rewarded with an appointment to a Los Angeles superior court judgeship in 1935, a post to which he was elected in the following year and reelected in 1942. Anxious for a more active political life, he became a public affairs commentator on a San Francisco radio station and a master of the media as well as an effective after-dinner speaker with a genial outgoing personality. In 1946 he was a beneficiary of a "musical chairs" political scenario that would ironically foreshadow a similar event with him as the victim twelve years later. Governor Warren's relations with the lieutenant governor, Frederick F. Houser, were less than amicable and the latter was persuaded to accept an appointment to a Los Angeles superior court judgeship in return for Judge Knight's agreeing to run for lieutenant governor with one of Warren's rare personal endorsements, an endorsement which probably helped him to an easy victory. Warren came to rue that decision as Knight ingratiated himself with the right wing of the Republican party and opposed Warren's liberal stands on several issues— health insurance, a fair employment practices commission, and the university oath controversy being the most prominent. Knight understandably was more disappointed than Warren with the latter's defeat for the vice presidency in 1948, and even considered running against him in the gubernatorial contest of 1950. In the end prudence prevailed, and Knight ran again for lieutenant governor and became the only candidate for that office in history who successfully crossfiled and won the office in the primary election. In 1953, of course, he was rewarded for his patience when he was automatically elevated to the governor's office when Warren resigned to join the Supreme Court.

Like the pragmatic politico that he was, Knight moved adroitly from the right wing of the Republican party toward the center in order to pick up as much of Warren's large following as possible. Stating his motto as "Moderation is best. Avoid all extremes," he called himself an Eisenhower Republican and took stands in favor of water resources development, air pollution control, increased benefits under the unemployment insurance, worker's compensation, mental health, and old-age pension programs, and the establishment of child-care centers for working mothers. Eventually he saw all of these proposals at least partially realized. He also gained widespread labor support when he opposed the enactment of a right-to-work law, which most labor leaders regarded as a euphemism for union busting. These tactics easily enabled him to win the gubernatorial election in 1954 against Richard Graves, the rather colorless Democratic candidate. In fact, he almost defeated Graves by cross-filing in the primary, an indication that his "nonpartisan" stance was succeeding well in capturing much of Warren's constituency. By 1958 when his proposed state budget totaled just under two billion dollars, he had seemingly refuted the Democrats' charge that he was a hidebound conservative and had positioned himself in the middle of the road to be able to make a powerful bid for reelection.

Trouble loomed for him from two quarters, however. One was from his rivals in the Republican party, Knowland and Nixon, who were aware that an attractive governor of California would be a strong contender for the presidency in 1960 when Eisenhower would be forced into retirement. Although neither admitted it, they had a mutual vested interest in "cutting him down to size" so that they could enhance their own designs upon the presidential office. Knight at first seemed to defend himself well against the two by refusing to endorse Nixon for the vice presidential renomination in 1956 and by getting an equal share of the delegates to the Republican national convention that year. The other threat came from the always dangerous right-wing members of the Republican party who mainly controlled its purse strings and who looked increasingly askance at Knight's departure from sacred conservative principles and at his efforts to cultivate the following of the hated Earl Warren.

In 1957 these two threats converged into one when Senator Knowland made the astounding announcement that he would not run for reelection the following year but would run for governor instead. He made it clear that he would wage a right-wing campaign in deliberate repudiation of Knight's posture when he heartily endorsed a very conservative right-to-work initiative which had qualified for the ballot and which Knight had emphatically opposed. When the stunned governor sought to fight back by contesting Knowland in the primary, he found that Nixon's associates were backing Knowland and that the party coffers would be closed to him by conservative Republican leaders who preferred Knowland and wished to avoid the "bloodletting" that would be sure to ensue if these two giants slugged it out in the primary election. The ludicrous outcome of the confrontation was another "musical chairs" event in which Knight agreed not to run for governor but to seek Knowland's vacated U.S. Senate seat instead.

It would be difficult to imagine a turn of events better calculated to bring disaster to the Republicans and a triumph for the delighted Democrats. Knight himself had charged that Knowland's sole motivation lay in using the governor's office as a stepping stone to the presidency, a charge constantly reiterated by the Democratic gubernatorial candidate, Edmund G. Brown. Brown also capitalized on Knowland's right-wing position to present himself as the pragmatic moderate in the Warren tradition, especially when he opposed the right-to-work initiative, which became increasingly unpopular as the campaign wore on. A host of other campaign mistakes, such as continued sniping between Knowland and Knight, were committed by the Republicans, causing one observer to wonder if they were attempting to commit political *hara-kiri.*

The result was the famous Democratic clean sweep of 1958. Not only did Brown defeat Knowland by more than a million votes, but the Democratic momentum was such (it was a Democratic election year nationwide also) that Knight was defeated for the U.S. Senate by Congressman Clair Engle, and the Democrats gained control of both houses of the legislature and all of the statewide constitutional offices except that of secretary of state. At long last the Republican monopoly on the state government had been destroyed. As one of life's ironies, it came about in part because Republican leaders deliberately chose to repudiate a well-known, capable, and electable incumbent governor in favor of a quixotic conservative who hardly had a chance.

Pat Brown and the Rise of the Democrats, 1952–1966

THERE WERE MORE REASONS for Edmund G. Brown's victory in 1958 than Republican ineptitude. The politically discerning could and did detect a steady increase in Democratic strength for a half-dozen years before the Republican rout of that year, and hindsight enables us to isolate at least three main causes of it: (1) the decline of crossfiling, (2) the rise of the California Democratic Council, and (3) the role and character of Brown himself.

Still in the doldrums at the beginning of the decade, the Democratic party held only one statewide office—Brown, himself, in the attorney general's chair—and the party presidential and senatorial races of 1952 were classics of incompetence. In the latter race Republican Senator William Knowland successfully crossfiled against a number of weak and divided Democratic opponents and deprived the party of a candidate in the fall election. In the presidential primary Attorney General Brown put together an uncommitted "free choice" slate of delegates to the national convention, but was frustrated by fellow Democrat

James Roosevelt, who bolted the ticket and organized a slate pledged to Senator Estes Kefauver of Tennessee, which won the election. This California delegation was in turn humiliated when Adlai Stevenson of Illinois captured the nomination, and the entire party was embarrassed when it made a wretched showing against the popular Republican candidate, Dwight Eisenhower, despite the fact that nearly sixty percent of the registered voters in the state were Democrats.

The year 1952, however, witnessed an event aiding the Democrats in the form of a crossfiling referendum passed by the voters in the general election. Although a Democratic-backed measure to abolish crossfiling entirely was rejected, the successful referendum did require crossfiling candidates to list their party affiliations after their names on the ballot, and hence alerted thousands of Democrats that they might be voting for Republicans and vice versa. The immediate effect was that the Democrats regained control of the nomination process in their party. In 1954 for the first time in forty years they fielded a complete slate of candidates for statewide and national offices instead of having crossfiling Republicans capture these nominations in the primary. The number of congressional seats that were won in the primary by crossfiled or unopposed candidates fell from 14 in 1952 to 2 in 1954. The number of contested seats in the state assembly at the same time rose from 18 to 58, and similar results took place in the state senate. The trend strengthened in subsequent years, and although the Republicans still continued to win most elective offices, they now had to wait until the general election to do so.

The California Democratic Council was organized to reverse these general-election results. Although representing nearly sixty percent of the state's registered voters since the mid-1930s, the Democrats were remarkably unable to translate that registration advantage into a polling advantage, and instead saw the Republicans consistently capture a bloc of Democratic voters and maintain control of the state government. As previously noted, the major reasons for Republican successes were crossfiling and the organization of the "private" Republican organization, the California Republican Assembly (CRA). It remained for the Democrats, having largely overcome the disadvantage of crossfiling, to take the next step and organize a Democratic counterpart of the CRA for the same purposes of coordinating party affairs and engaging in preprimary endorsements. This is what the California Democratic Council (CDC) did, and for a decade it did so brilliantly. Founded mainly by state senators George Miller and Richard Richards and by Alan Cranston, a journalist and future state Controller and U.S. senator, the CDC grew out of a grass-roots Democratic club movement (especially many Adlai Stevenson clubs in 1952), and was officially "born" as a statewide organization at a Democratic meeting in Fresno in November 1953. It selected and endorsed candidates for practically every partisan elective office in the state in 1954 and 1956, and had the ineffable satisfaction of seeing them all win in the primaries and an increasing number of them win in the general elections as well. This was especially true of the state legislature where the Republican majority in the assembly shrank from a 53-27 edge in 1952 to 42-38 in 1956, and from a 29-11 edge in the senate to an even 20-20 split. When Democratic senator Hugh Burns of Fresno picked up two Republican votes and got himself elected as president pro-tem of the senate in 1957, many Democrats could anticipate a victory for Brown the next year with a considerable degree of realism.

Brown himself played no small part in this Democratic emergence and triumph. An "old pol" who helped to keep the party in existence during its lean years, Brown had been in politics in one way or another practically all his life. Nicknamed "Pat" for Patrick Henry after delivering an enthusiastic high-school speech in support of a Liberty Bond sale during World War I, Brown became a San Francisco lawyer and ran, as a Republican, for the state assembly in 1928 at the age of twenty-three. Failing to get elected, he went back into private practice but involved himself in local governmental affairs throughout the 1930s. Changing his party registration to Democratic in 1934, he became an enthusiastic New Dealer and ran for district attorney in San Francisco in 1939. He failed again but succeeded on his second try in 1943. He held that office until 1950, was nominated but not elected to the state attorney generalship in 1946, but was elected to that office on his second attempt in 1950. As the only Democrat holding statewide office, he was the party's elder statesman by default, and when he successfully crossfiled for reelection in 1954 he gained additional status because he was the first Democratic candidate for statewide office ever to do this. Unlike some other Democratic "professionals" he was friendly, or at least neutral, toward the "amateurs" in the CDC, and as attorney general he performed some important party services. He successfully opposed an effort to destroy the 160-acre limitation[1] regarding federal irrigation water in the state, and in 1958 he used his authority to entitle Proposition 18 "Employer and Employee Relations" instead of "Right to Work" as its sponsors wanted. After a career of many reverses, his sweeping victory of that year gave him a chance at long last to utilize his experience and to act on his principles.

He was not slow in making the effort. Calling in his inaugural address for a program of "responsible liberalism," Brown invoked the spirit of progressive governors nationwide from Charles Evans Hughes to Earl Warren, the latter with whom he was closely associated and from whom he had learned much. Although he possessed none of Warren's remarkable charisma, he rivaled him in experience and pragmatic political ability, especially in working with people of differing parties and differing beliefs, and in the arts of compromise. He knew the value of "striking while the iron is hot," and he immediately called for a long list of reform legislation while still bearing the aura of a huge popular mandate from the recent election. The result of this combination of circumstances was that the 1959 legislature enacted some 35 of the 40 major legislative proposals that the governor submitted or supported, a record that compares favorably with that of any previous governor, Warren and Johnson included.

Many of these enactments were expansions of existing programs, such as increased welfare payments, old-age pensions, minimum wages, workers' social insurance benefits, expanded school and highway construction programs, and enlarged higher education budgets. Others, such as consumer protection and smog control, were newer but relatively limited in scope. But still other aspects of Brown's 1959 program were innovative and profound in their impact upon the state at large. Some would place the law ending crossfiling in that category, but that was probably in reality anticlimactic, as crossfiling had already been seriously crippled by the 1952 referendum. More pervasive were the two legislative breakthroughs in the fields of race relations and water.

Warren, it will be remembered, had called for the establishment of a fair employment practices commission as early as 1945, but nothing came of it during his administration nor during that of his successor. Brown resubmitted the proposal to the legislature and browbeat key legislators on its behalf until it was passed. The result was that it henceforth became illegal for employers and labor unions to discriminate in hiring and admissions practices on the basis of race, and a state agency, the Division of Fair Employment Practices, was set up to enforce the law. Brown also pushed through a bill outlawing racial discrimination in restaurants, other public accommodations, and publicly assisted housing projects, and by so doing helped to put the state in the vanguard of the "civil rights revolution" that was forming in the nation.

Often regarded as Brown's chief claim to fame is the passage of the Burns-Porter water bonds act of 1959. With the enormous growth of southern California since the 1880s, the population pattern had grown increasingly "out of sync" with the state's natural setting. The dry southern region came to possess many more people than its water supply could support, while the wet northern region produced a water surplus and was often bedeviled by disasters caused by flooding. While pure reason might decree that the problem be solved by moving the people to the water, the dynamics of demography in southern California was to do the opposite—utilize the awesome panoply of civil engineering technology, dams, canals, pumping stations, siphons, tunnels, and the like to move the water to the people. While technologically feasible, it had long proved politically impossible to develop and implement a comprehensive state water plan of this sort—the Central Valley Project was of limited scope—because of sectional rivalries between north and south. Brown was able to break this impasse in the legislature with the passage of a $1.75 billion bond issue to begin financing the comprehensive "Caifornia Water Plan." The plan guaranteed the north sufficient water for its needs and the south a sufficient share of the surplus to win its support, and was approved by the people in a special election in 1960. The first phase of the

plan was inaugurated by the construction of the giant Oroville
Dam and since 1973 the project has been supplying the southern part of the state with about a million acre-feet of water
annually. When completed the project will divert more than
two million acre-feet southward. Nowadays many criticize the
project as a contributor to the environmental crisis in the state,
but whatever its ecological inadequacies, it must be reckoned a
political achievement of a high order.

Needless to say, these legislative enactments cost money, and
Brown was forced to grasp the nettles of taxes and budget. The
budget surplus (Warren's famous "rainy day fund") had dis-
appeared during Knight's administration, and it was an open
secret that the California citizen was in for a round of new and
increased taxation. Using the tried-and-true strategy of raising
taxes in his first year as governor in hopes that his constituents
might have forgotten about it by his fourth, Brown called for
increased levies on incomes, inheritances, banks, insurance
companies, corporations, race tracks, and beer, and for new
levies on cigarettes, cigars, and oil extraction (the severance
tax). Although a legislative donnybrook occurred over the
issue, all of the governor's tax proposals were passed except for
those on cigars and oil, the latter rejection reflecting the peren-
nial political muscle of the oil lobby and arousing the governor's
articulate but ineffective ire. With new revenues came increased
expenditures, and Brown's budgets rose from $2.2 billion in
1959 to almost $5 billion by 1966. Clearly Brown had placed
himself in the fiscal tradition of progressive governors such as
C. C. Young and Earl Warren, and he argued, as they had, that
the massive population growth that characterized the 1950s and
1960s necessitated increased governmental expenditures, and
that all the responsible executive could promise his constituents
was their money's worth in state services, not reduced taxes.

After his triumphs of 1959 the governor suffered a couple of
humiliating, but not fatal, setbacks in 1960. Widely publicized,
but of marginal importance, was the Chessman case. Caryl
Chessman, convicted of a brutal sex crime in Los Angeles and
sentenced to death, had protested his innocence and fought off
innumerable execution dates by legal maneuvers and publicity
ploys (he smuggled two books into print while in San Quentin).
Brown, a principled opponent of capital punishment and sub-

jected to enormous pressure from many groups who made Chessman's case a cause célèbre, vacillated on the issue, granted stays, sought unsuccessfully to shift the responsibility to the legislature, and finally allowed the execution to take place. He satisfied no one in this incident and gave the appearance of being weak and indecisive, an impression that was furthered by his involvement in presidential politics that year.

Putting together a favorite-son delegation to the national Democratic convention made up of delegates partial to one leading candidate or another (especially John F. Kennedy, Adlai Stevenson, and Lyndon Johnson), Brown succeeded in dissuading those candidates from fielding slates of their own, but his slate had no unity or coherence whatsoever. Vice President Richard Nixon sought to embarrass Brown by declaring that if Brown got more votes for his slate than Nixon did for his, it would suggest a repudiation of the nation's tough anti-Communist stand and that "Chou En-lai will take it as the first step by the United States in the admission of Red China to the U.N."[2] While this flagrant red-baiting reveals how far Nixon had to travel on his road to the "opening" with China in 1971, it helped to serve his purposes, for he did poll more votes than Brown in the presidential primaries. This was largely attributable to the fact that the leader of the old-age pension lobby in California, George McLain, entered the Democratic primary against Brown and polled an amazing 600,000 votes. At the Democratic convention Brown lost further status when he was unable to control the delegation, which fragmented in support of four different candidates, and refused to follow Brown and swing into line behind John F. Kennedy when his nomination became assured. This may have been prophetic of the fall election when Kennedy eventually lost the state by a mere 36,000 votes.

Brown bounced back from the reverses of 1960, however, and secured the passage of three additional major pieces of legislation over the next year, two of them in the field of higher education. The Master Plan law of 1960 rationalized the three main postsecondary education institutions— the community colleges, the state colleges (now called the State University and College system), and the University of California— into a comprehensive format with clearly defined roles for each. It enabled the state also to take a giant step toward its expressed ideal of providing the opportunity for a low-cost college education to every California citizen who could profit by one (as well as for many who could not, cynics added). The Fisher Act of 1961 upgraded the state's teacher education system by requiring every candidate for a teaching credential to have a genuine academic major, rather than allowing them to major in "education" as had been the practice.

Also in 1961 Brown badgered the legislature into tackling the complex problem of government reorganization. This, it will be recalled, had been among the proudest achievements of progressive governors William D. Stephens and C. C. Young in the 1920s, but by the 1960s so many new governmental agencies had been haphazardly created, that it needed to be done over again. Attacking this administrative hodgepodge, Brown and the legislature eventually reorganized it into eight major agencies and two departments, and although conservatives attacked the system as "supergovernment," its advantages in terms of greater efficiency and cost accountability soon became apparent to all. This time, furthermore, the reorganization impetus did not stop at the executive department but carried over into the legislature as well. Two main factors largely account for this: the reapportionment revolution and Jesse Unruh.

Assemblyman Jesse Unruh was Brown's strong right arm throughout much of his administration. As chairman of the Ways and Means Committee and, after 1961, as speaker of the assembly, he was in a position to make or break Brown's legislative program, and he usually not only made it but went on to secure the passage of a number of "Unruh Acts" of his own. A master of the techniques of pressuring special-interest groups to donate campaign money, which he dubbed the "the mother's milk of politics," he soon became unbeatable in his assembly district and thereby in a position to deflect funding from such groups to the election campaigns of fellow legislators who did him the service of voting "right." The existence of the "Grateful to Jesse for Mentioning Me to the Men with the Money Club" was at least one cause of the legislative magic that Unruh was often able to perform. He was, however, more than a political wheeler-dealer. Genuinely interested in upgrading the quality of the legislature, he secured the passage of laws that enormously expanded legislative staffs and enhanced the general level of the legislature's performance to the extent that it soon came to be rated by political scientists as the best in the nation. A 1966 constitutional amendment providing for annual, general, year-round sessions and for legislative salaries commensurate with other professions and geared to the cost of living has further enhanced the professional character of the legislature and perhaps contributed to Unruh's receiving the George Washington Award from the American Good Government Society in 1967.

The reapportionment issue also had profound effects upon the legislature. As governor, Earl Warren had stoutly defended California's "federal plan" of a deliberately nonrepresentative state senate offset by a popularly representative assembly, but as Chief Justice he ruled in 1962 that such apportionment systems were unconstitutional. Although conservative and rural interests fought the decision strenuously, they eventually were forced to succumb, and in 1965 the state senate traumatically reapportioned itself. Some twenty-two senators were retired to private life, and the eight counties of southern California gained the same control over the senate that they already exercised over the assembly. The old breed of senators, perennially reelected from their sparsely populated and personally controlled districts and entrenched into powerful seignories in the legislative power structure, were replaced by a new breed of constituent-oriented political technicians representing complex urban districts. Although some valuable traditions may have been lost, the process of professionalization of the legislature was probably enhanced by the change.

By 1962 Brown, exhausted by the pace he had set, seriously considered retiring to private life. But when Richard Nixon, seeking to make a political comeback after his bare failure to win the presidency in 1960, announced his candidacy for governor and attacked Brown for "the mess in Sacramento," Brown's war-horse instincts were aroused and he decided to run for reelection. The result was one of the nastier gubernatorial campaigns in a state that is certainly no stranger to such encounters. Nixon, having himself been attacked by right-wing opponents in the primary, used similar tactics against Brown, suggesting that he was somehow failing to protect the state from a vague

Communist or radical menace. He also revealed himself to be rather unfamiliar with, and sometimes even uninterested in, many of the state's problems, and Brown again used the "stepping stone to the presidency" charge with devastating effectiveness. In the general election he decisively defeated Nixon and, since he had successively beaten the two leading Republicans in the state (Knowland and Nixon), he began to acquire the reputation of a giant-killer.[3] The Democrats continued their domination of the partisan constitutional offices (again, all except the secretary of state) and the state legislature, although by slightly smaller margins. Only their failure to defeat moderate Republican U.S. Senator Thomas Kuchel in his bid for reelection and their loss of the nonpartisan office of superintendent of public instruction to conservative Republican Max Rafferty kept the Democrats from making a clean sweep. So solidly entrenched were the Democrats in Sacramento and so seemingly able to translate their party registration strength into voting strength that it seemed to many that California was in for a period of Democratic dominance at least as long as the sixty-year era of Republican dominance preceding it.

These beliefs proved to be profound illusions. Instead, the Democratic triumph of 1962 was turned into a Democratic decline in 1963, '64, and '65, and into a Democratic disaster in 1966. At first the administration seemed stronger than ever, especially when the legislature passed the Rumford Act of 1963, which outlawed racial discrimination in the sale of houses, over the strenuous opposition of the real estate lobby. Soon, however, the searing conflicts of the sixties began tearing California Democrats apart. The uprisings on the college campuses, especially at Berkeley, which were foreshadowed by the student protests against the House Committee on Un-American Activities hearings at San Francisco in 1960 and culminated in a paralyzing mass demonstration on the Berkeley campus in late 1964, began the process of polarizing the party into antagonistic camps. Brown found himself castigated by student activists and left-wingers for using the Highway Patrol to arrest striking students and condemned by conservatives for not using sufficient force against them. Soon the nation's deepening involvement in the Vietnam War exacerbated these conflicts, especially within the CDC.

The 1964 elections foreshadowed the decline. Although President Lyndon Johnson easily carried the state against Senator Barry Goldwater, he did so by a smaller margin than in the nation at large, and a similar decline in the Democratic vote for the state assembly (a very sensitive indicator of voting trends) was recorded. More damaging were two upheavals over the U.S. Senate race and a quarrel over the repeal of the Rumford Act. When Senator Clair Engle's ultimately fatal illness took him out of the race, a contest arose among several prominent Democrats over who should succeed him, a conflict seemingly contained by the CDC which endorsed State Controller Alan Cranston and induced the other contenders to withdraw. At the last minute, however, San Franciscan Pierre Salinger, President Kennedy's former press secretary, entered the race and won the Democratic nomination in a bitterly contested primary election. Salinger in turn went down to defeat against conservative Republican George Murphy, the former Hollywood actor and song and dance performer. Salinger's defeat was largely attributable to his strong opposition to Proposition 14, a constitutional amendment backed by the real estate lobby which sought repeal of the Rumford Act and other state restrictions upon the disposal of private property. The proposition passed easily, angering blacks and liberals (Brown bluntly labeled it a vote for bigotry) and creating the conditions of the "white backlash" against desegregation legislation, which the Republicans could exploit. In 1965 and 1966 the Watts riots and other racial upheavals plus the furious conflict over the Vietnam War further shattered the Democratic coalition. Brown, seeking to maintain amicable relations with the national administration, tried to dampen the controversy by inducing the CDC to adopt a moderate stand on the Vietnam issue. Eventually he forced the dismissal of Simon Casady, president of the CDC, for his outspoken opposition to the war, but it was a pyrrhic victory. The CDC was shattered into permanent impotence, and the liberal wing of the party was so embittered against Brown that many refused to support him in his reelection bid.

While the Democrats were tearing themselves apart, the Republicans were putting themselves together again. After their grievous losses in 1958 and 1962 the Republicans too had been torn by factionalism, especially by the rise of what came to be called the "radical right." Spokesmen of this persuasion were more than mere extreme conservatives such as Barry Goldwater or William Knowland. They were more reminiscent of Joseph McCarthy or Jack Tenney in their tendency to attack liberals and moderates as not only "wrong" but as subversives or traitors. The most notorious in this regard were the "Birchers" or members of the John Birch Society, which was organized by Robert Welch in Massachusetts in 1958 and took deep root in southern California in the years afterward. The Birchers and their associates became entrenched in the Republican party, particularly in 1962 when they elected two Birchers to Congress and strongly supported gubernatorial candidate Joseph Shell, who was a militant conservative though not an extremist, against Richard Nixon whom they distrusted. Nixon attacked the Birchers (which did not prevent him from appropriating some of their tactics in his subsequent campaign against Brown), but was unsuccessful in having them purged from the party. Instead, after Nixon's defeat they and their right-wing supporters took control of the Republican volunteer organizations—the Young Republicans, the CRA, and eventually a new pro-Goldwater organization, the United Republicans of California (UROC).

The Birch crowd did not take over the official Republican party, however. Ironically, the Democrats in the legislature saved the party from this fate by passing a law in 1964 allowing the moderates and conservatives to pack the state central committee.[4] The result was a standoff between the radical right extremists and a new group of professional managers and technicians ("IBM types," one study calls them) who were far less interested in ideological combat than in organization, funding, and winning elections.[5] Recognizing their need of each other, the two groups agreed not to engage in mutual recrimination and bloodletting, but to concentrate instead upon the common enemy, the Democrats. The guiding genius of this reconciliation policy was the newly elected (1964) state party chairman, Gaylord Parkinson, a southern California doctor, who issued an edict which he called the "eleventh commandment" and which others called "Parkinson's law." It stated: "Thou shalt speak no evil of other Republicans," and it served admirably to keep Republicans from each other's throats during primary election campaigns.

The 1966 Republican primary demonstrated its feasibility. San Francisco mayor George Christopher was the choice of the moderates, while the darling of the right and also of the "technicians" was the Hollywood and television actor Ronald Reagan. The two candidates managed to keep their knives sheathed even after a couple of close calls. One occurred when Reagan curiously concluded that Christopher had impugned his integrity at a joint appearance early in the campaign and the other when Christopher became convinced that the Reagan camp was the source of scurrilous charges that Christopher was an "ex-convict" as a result of being prosecuted for technical violations of federal milk purity laws when he was in the dairy business years before. The former incident came to naught when Reagan's temper cooled and the latter also when Christopher discovered that the Democrats were responsible for exposing his "criminal record." The Democrats had leaked the news because they had concluded that Christopher, as an experienced politician, would be more difficult to defeat in the general election than the "amateur" Reagan. When Reagan easily won in the primary, the Democrats had adequate opportunity to test that theory.

The Democratic primary, on the other hand, was a bare-knuckled donnybrook from the start. Brown, already under fire from the anti–Vietnam War Democrats, had by this time broken with Jesse Unruh. Their rivalry had surfaced in 1964 when Brown backed Cranston for U.S. senator, and Unruh, long a Kennedy partisan, supported Salinger. Unruh was visibly angry when Brown announced his intention to run for a third term instead of leaving the way clear for him, Unruh, to run. Although he announced his support for Brown, he did not campaign for him and instead found urgent business in several foreign countries that required his personal attention.[6] To complicate matters further Mayor Samuel Yorty of Los Angeles, a curious combination of New Dealer and red-baiter, entered the primary against Brown. Although Brown won the election, Yorty took some 900,000 votes away from him and showed Brown's vulnerability in the fall election, for those 900,000 votes were now "up for grabs."

Reagan apparently grabbed them and a few others besides. An absolute master of the electronic media, especially television

via which most of the campaign was conducted, Reagan projected a poised, articulate, magnetic, "nice guy" image of himself that seemed a visible refutation of the extremist image
which Brown sought to portray of him. His smooth campaign,
managed by the reputable Spencer-Roberts firm of campaign
consultants, even capitalized on his political inexperience by
suggesting that California needed a "citizen-politician" instead
of a "professional" politician such as Brown who typified
"machine politics" and spendthrift liberalism. His oft-reiterated
set speech mouthed the glories of traditional ideological conservatism—free enterprise, attacks on ultraliberals reputedly on
college campuses, reduced taxes, reduced budgets, and reduced
scope of governmental activity—and the state was in a conservative mood. The Rumford Act was again an issue as the state
supreme court had declared the repeal initiative of 1964 unconstitutional, and Reagan advocated changing the Rumford
law because it interfered with "sacred" property rights. Brown
charged that Reagan was exploiting the white backlash, but
voters seemed to believe that Reagan's stand acquitted him of
racism and safeguarded the rights of private property at the
same time.

When the votes were counted Reagan not only had won by
993,000 votes, but the Republicans had also swept every other
state constitutional office except that of attorney general, and
reduced the comfortable Democratic majorities in both houses
of the legislature to very thin margins (21-19 in the senate and
42-38 in the assembly). After eight years in office Edmund G.
Brown, perhaps the last of the old-time progressive governors,
a "giant-killer" who had laid low two of the most prominent
Republicans in the state and nation, went down to defeat at the
hands of a show-business celebrity who had never before run
for public office.

CHAPTER FIVE

The Reagan Administration

RONALD REAGAN came to the governor's office with some definite ideas in mind. Although mainly negative—reducing the scope and cost of government, curbing rebellious and radical students and professors, cutting the crime rate, and forcing welfare "cheats" and "spongers" off the relief roles— these ideas were nevertheless expected to be the main motive forces in determining policy. Ideology, in short, was deliberately designed to replace pragmatism in the administration of public affairs. It could hardly be otherwise since the pragmatic approach emphasizes impartial studies of situations and experience at the expense of doctrinaire values, and Reagan was a committed right-wing doctrinaire with no political experience whatsoever. In his inaugural address of January 1967 he pledged himself to a policy of "cut, squeeze, and trim" in order to reduce the cost of government, an objective that he repeatedly asserted was his number one priority throughout his administration. Californians could seemingly look forward to an administration that would systematically act on ideological principles rather than grope for solutions to problems as the problems occurred.

At first the governor looked as if he would fulfill the conservative promise in the 1967 legislative session. Calling dramatically for a straight ten percent reduction of the state budget, he infuriated liberals by seeking even deeper cuts in what they considered their most inviolable programs. He slashed the higher

education budget by several millions and persuaded the Regents
of the University of California to increase student fees and to fire
the university president, Clark Kerr, whose name had become
anathema among conservatives for coddling student demonstra-
tors. He implemented cuts (which were later in the year invalidated by the state supreme court) in the Medi-Cal program, a
1966 federal and state program to assist the "medically indigent"
with their medical bills. And he vetoed a bill to "pass on" Social
Security payment increases to recipients of state old-age pensions.

His most controversial economy measure, however, was his
cutting of the mental health budget. The Short-Doyle Act of
1959 was considered another progressive achievement of the
Edmund G. Brown administration (although more a legislative
product rather than a executive one) because it substituted for
the process of "warehousing" the mentally ill in large state
institutions one of treating them and releasing those showing
improvement for additional treatment in mental health clinics in
their home communities.[1] Since many patients could live productive lives while undergoing such treatment, and since their
departure from the state mental hospitals enabled the staff there
to concentrate on the more severe cases of mental disability, the
program was considered an enlightened one. The reduction in
caseload, however, caused Reagan to believe that he could
correspondingly reduce hospital staffs, despite the fact that the
higher turnover of patients and greater degree of mental impair-
ment of the resident population suggested that more rather than
less staff was needed. Nevertheless, Reagan infuriated many
mental-health people when he proceeded to lay off some 3,700
institutional employees (he eventually settled for about 2,600),
and called for the closing of some outpatient clinics which had
made possible the reduction in patient load in the hospitals in
the first place! Although this decision eventually boomeranged
to his disadvantage, it and other enactments (a law providing
stiffer penalties for violent crimes, for example) convinced
many that Reagan was acting out his conservative ideology with
perfect consistency.

Others, however, were not so sure. After his early call for a
ten percent cut, Reagan found that the budget was largely made
up of fixed costs, federally mandated programs, enduring com-

mitments, and adjustments for inflation, all of which made a net reduction politically if not economically impossible. Consequently his 1967–1968 budget totaled just over $5 billion, a $400 million increase over that of the previous year. Unpalatable as it was, it was a foretaste of things to come. Every subsequent budget, despite his heroic efforts to "cut, squeeze, and trim," would increase accordingly, and the budget would more than double during his tenure, passing the $10 billion mark in his last year in office. Like other governors before him, Reagan found that increased budgets meant increased taxes, and although he blamed the empty treasury, with some justification, upon the Brown administration, he "bit the bullet" and signed a law that increased taxes by almost $1 billion, the largest tax increase in the history of any state.

Equally disillusioning to his right-wing adherents was the governor's role in the effort to repeal the Rumford fair housing law. After calling for repeal in the election campaign, he failed to endorse the repeal bill in the legislature until it had been amended beyond recognition, and when it failed of passage he attacked those who demanded an "all or nothing" solution to the problem. Conservatives fumed but liberals (silently) cheered. Finally, the governor's successful demand for legislation to protect the middle fork of the Feather River revealed him to be more of a moderate on the conservation issue than many of his supporters and opponents had expected.

By the end of 1967 Ronald Reagan had walked a familiar path in California politics. The occupant of the right had moved toward the middle of the road; the spokesman for extremism had become the practitioner of moderation; the ideologue had seemingly become a pragmatic politician. All of California's governors since the 1920s, if they were not committed pragmatists at the start, had made this shift in some degree and all for the same reason. Reality is always more complex than ideology, and contrary evidence and opposing opinions, which can be combatted or ignored by the office-seeker, must be accommodated and compromised with by the office-holder. In the process of governing the ideologist risks forfeiting the advantage that brought him to power—the appearance of being above politics and an exemplar of untarnished principle. His reiterations of hallowed principles begin to ring hollowly in the ears of his followers who then regard him as a sell-out and seek other messiahs who, they hope, will not compromise virtue for sordid political gain.

The remarkable thing about Reagan is that he escaped this fate. In spite of these compromises and many more to come, he kept his image unspotted in the eyes of his disciples as the great conservative, the great economizer, the great nonpolitician, through eight years in the governor's chair, and he keeps it yet today. There are probably two main reasons for this astounding achievement. The first is that his image has some basis in reality: Reagan did not become a dedicated practical politician. Openly contemptuous of legislators and disdainful of the legislative process, he minimized his contact with political figures and associated mainly with friends from Hollywood and the world of big business. Bored not only with the workaday world of politics, he was also surprisingly disinterested in the details of the main political issues of the day. Unlike most professional politicians who immersed themselves in a veritable ocean of political facts and opinions and constantly discussed them with their colleagues and rivals (both Pat Brown and Jesse Unruh are good examples), Reagan used his acting experience and retentive memory to make a "quick study" of an issue, make a decision on it, and go on to the next problem. He surrounded himself with a corps of able assistants, whose main function was allegedly to compile one-page "mini-memos" on issues of the day, and Reagan's typical day in office was to run through these, either accept or reject the proposed solutions, and be home for dinner by six o'clock. His home life was a happy one, and on weekends he habitually fled the Sacramento scene with his wife and child to their "real" home in the Malibu hills near Los Angeles.

This system, while superficially efficient, was also a kind of institutionalization of ignorance in office. Reagan's grasp of the ramifications of his policies was often shown to be remarkably shallow and oftentimes nonexistent. One of the more favorably disposed students of his administration notes that he had "the advantage of a practically photographic memory and the disadvantage of a short memory span," and reporters at televised press conferences were constantly surprised at how often he answered questions with a disarmingly candid "I don't know."[2]

To be sure, such conferences also revealed him at his best with original wit, snappy one-liners, and bantering good humor. His wit could be caustic—"their signs said 'Make love, not war,' but they didn't look like they could do either," he said of a hostile student demonstration—but it could also be cruel or at least crassly insensitive. When he was told that many San Francisco poor folk were accepting the free food that Patricia Hearst's kidnappers had forced her father to hand out, he sighed for an "outbreak of botulism" to teach them a lesson.

Unquestionably, it was this gifted handling of the media, especially television, that was the second and more important reason for the maintenance of Reagan's image. In this respect Reagan exemplifies a profoundly revolutionary reality of our times, the power of television to anaesthetize memory. Mundane political facts can easily be obscured by a master of the media projecting a positive image of himself while presumably interpreting these facts. While Reagan's checkered record with the legislature was being compiled he was constantly on the speaker's platform and in the television studio preaching the gospel of conservatism and the merits of "cut, squeeze, and trim" with magical effectiveness. Ignoring his large budget and tax increases, he regaled his audiences with examples of his "economies." Most were more symbolic than significant— temporary halts in building projects, using former Governor Brown's office stationery with his name blotted out, disarming toll collectors on bridge and selling their revolvers—but Reagan more than any other politician of the television era understood the power of symbols. The result was that at the very time that he was establishing a record as a politician and pragmatist he was sharpening an image of himself as a nonpolitician and ideologue on the state and national scene.[3]

His interest in establishing a national reputation soon became evident, for 1968 was a presidential election year. Though his bid for the Republican presidential nomination was frustrated by Richard Nixon's well organized and successful campaign, it gained him national recognition and probably contributed to his party's success in the state elections. The Democrats and their titular leader, Jesse Unruh, were apparently so benumbed by Robert Kennedy's assassination in Los Angeles that fateful year that Unruh failed to conduct any kind of concerted campaign for his party's state and national candidates. The result was that the Republicans carried the state for Nixon. In line with a Reagan-backed and party-sponsored "Cal-plan," they gained control of the state legislature as well. The only Republican "setback" was in the U.S. Senate race. In the primary the moderate and effective incumbent, Thomas Kuchel, had been upset by the flamboyant right-winger Max Rafferty, the state superintendent of public instruction. The Reagan forces, apparently uneasy over the possibility of their hero's having to share the limelight with another dynamic conservative who could rival him in showmanship and surpass him in demagoguery, deliberately failed to support Rafferty and perhaps viewed his defeat at the hands of the Democrats' Alan Cranston with some relief. Both Kuchel and Rafferty were threatening to Reagan, the former because he was too liberal and the latter because he was too conservative. Now they were both gone.

Gone also was the Republican excuse that the party could not implement Reagan's program because of Democratic domination of the legislature. Ironically, 1969 and 1970, the two years that Reagan's party controlled the legislature (41 seats to 39 in the assembly and 21 to 19 in the senate) were the least productive in an administration already strikingly undistinguished for legislative productivity. In part this inactivity reflected the internecine quarrels among the Republicans, particularly in the state senate. At first the Republicans in that body voted to retain Hugh Burns as president pro-tempore because he was as conservative as any Republican. In May 1969 a moderate group rebelled and elected Republican Howard Way to replace Burns, but in February 1970 a ludicrous coalition of conservative Republicans and liberal Democrats unseated Way and replaced him with Jack Schrade, whose extreme conservatism was exceeded only by his parliamentary ineptitude. Democratic obstructionism no doubt also played a part in the legislative barrenness of those years, but it was also attributable to the essentially negative attitude of the Reagan Republicans toward government and public policy. A party that thinks government is already too big and too costly is unlikely to propose new programs to deal with public problems. Instead Reagan dedicated himself to the reform of such programs by reducing rather than expanding their scope.

Some of this negativism in the environmental field was applauded by ecologists and liberals. This was especially true of Reagan's veto of the Round Valley Dam project which would have flooded a beautiful pastoral setting in the Eel River valley and displaced the Yuki Indians whose ancient culture reached far back into the prehistoric era. But Reagan's main efforts were directed toward reform of the various social service programs of the state, and since in his mind reform of these programs was synonymous with their reduction or even elimination, he raised howls of anguish from the traditional liberals in the state. By 1969 he had abandoned his campaign against the Department of Mental Hygiene and even restored some cuts already made, but the welfare and Medi-Cal programs in his opinion needed the budgetary scalpel (always referred to as a meat-axe by opponents).

To his consternation Reagan found that his opponents in welfare reform were not only Democrats but also Nixon Republicans in the federal Department of Health, Education, and Welfare (HEW). His own running mate of 1966, Lieutenant Governor Robert Finch, now headed that agency, while his undersecretary was former California state senator John G. Veneman, a Republican moderate whom Reagan disliked. The president believed that the best way to reform welfare was to adopt a Family Assistance Plan, a cash grant, guaranteed annual income program for poverty-stricken family heads, employed or unemployed. The plan was anathema to right-wing Republicans such as Reagan who sought to reduce welfare caseloads by tightening eligibility requirements, thereby eliminating the "undeserving" from the welfare rolls and confining and possibly expanding welfare payments to the "truly needy." Reagan was furious when HEW announced that it would hold hearings to determine whether California's failure to grant cost-of-living increases to welfare recipients would make the state ineligible to receive almost a billion dollars in federal matching funds in 1970. He avoided the federal cuts, but his welfare reform bill failed in the legislature that year, and a number of his attempted cuts in the Medi-Cal program were overruled in the courts. Also, in

1970 he was whipsawed into signing a Social Security "pass-on" bill after a tearful confrontation with an aged pensioner at a televised political rally, one of the few times in his career when he was disadvantaged by television exposure. To add to his catalogue of woes, an economic recession of that year brought the state budget out of balance and forced the governor to ask the legislature for a tax increase in a year when he was seeking reelection. This embarrassment was intensified when his tax bill was defeated by one vote in the state senate and that vote was cast by a member of his own party, Clark Bradley.

Not surprisingly the governor entered his reelection campaign in 1970 in a weaker position than in 1966. Fortunately, his opponent was worse off. Jesse Unruh captured the Democratic nomination, but ironically the once great fund-raiser now suffered a famine of "mother's milk." His high-handed refusal to support Brown four years previously and other Democrats in 1968 now came home to haunt him, and the party coffers remained closed. Even so, he waged a creditable campaign as Reagan defeated him by only about half as many votes as the number by which he bested Brown, and Reagan shocked many Republican candidates by his inability to carry them into office on his political coat-tails. Reagan was unable to purge a number of "willful" Democratic state senators who had blocked his tax reform proposals. Instead, the Republicans lost control of the legislature (21 to 19 in the senate and 43 to 37 in the assembly), and thereby forfeited the chance to apportion the state to their advantage after the census of 1970. A foretaste of things to come was the Republican loss of the secretaryship of state to Edmund G. Brown, Jr., and, most shocking of all, Reagan's old friend Senator George Murphy lost in his bid for reelection to a young congressman, John H. Tunney. All things considered, Jesse Unruh's defensive boast that the Democrats had "cut off his [Reagan's] coat-tails clear up to the lapels" was perhaps justifiable hyperbole.

The year 1971 was for Reagan a year of frustration and triumph. Deterred from making deep cuts in the welfare budget, he watched helplessly as the overall state budget rose to nearly $6.8 billion despite his item vetoes of more than $400 million. Furthermore, the economic recession caused a projected revenue shortfall, confronting him with the two most grisly alternatives that an ideological conservative can face: an unbalanced budget or a tax increase. The governor grimaced and accepted the latter, the 1971 tax law raising more than a half-billion dollars of additional revenue through revisions of capital gains and corporation tax laws and, more sensationally, through the adoption of the withholding method of collecting the state income tax. Reagan had always taken an ideological stand against withholding by uttering the famous dictum that "taxes should hurt." By this he meant that if taxes were collected by the relatively painless method of withholding them from citizens' paychecks, the taxpayers would be less inclined to feel the pinch and object to their government's "extravagance." Proponents argued that the lump sun method of payment also enabled many citizens to escape the "hurt" entirely by failing to file returns or by leaving the state before they were due, thereby depriving the state of an estimated $100 million in lost revenues. In the fiscal pinch of 1971 Reagan again allowed pragmatism to prevail over ideology and signed the withholding measure into law.

In a political sense, the setbacks the governor suffered over fiscal matters were more than compensated for by the passage of the welfare reform act. Sometimes referred to as the Reagan-Moretti Act, the order of the names should probably be reversed, for it was the Democratic speaker of the assembly, Robert Moretti, who initiated conferences with Reagan and his staff out of which the new law emerged. Reagan, on the other hand, had fought for the principle of caseload reduction through tightened eligibility requirements against President Nixon's Family Assistance Plan, and when the latter failed in Congress the momentum was in favor of the Reagan approach. Reagan and Moretti learned to respect one another, although the governor continued to regard the speaker as a spendthrift, and Moretti became convinced that Reagan was largely lacking in compassion for the plight of welfare recipients. Both men made concessions, and the end result was clearly a compromise. In return for more stringent eligibility requirements to receive aid under the Aid to Families with Dependent Children (AFDC) program, a work requirement system for able-bodied welfare recipients, and reduced Medi-Cal costs by expanding a "prepaid" medical insurance system, Reagan had to surrender on his "closed end" and "equitable apportionment" funding schemes which would fix state welfare expenditures at a predetermined level regardless of caseload increases or other increased costs. Reagan exulted, nevertheless, that the new law "achieves what we sought from the beginning," and when caseloads declined in the following years and several other states copied the law, the governor's image as a hero who slew (or at least crippled) the welfare "monster" was firmly fixed in the public mind.

Second thoughts on the law tend to revise this image a bit, however. The welfare caseload reductions were probably largely attributable to the economic upturn which was already under way when the act went into effect. The job placement program for the able-bodied recipients turned out to be totally ineffectual and was subsequently discontinued. The prepaid medical care program proved likewise ineffective and sometimes scandalously so. Some of the antifraud provisions were at least partly effective, but others were successfully challenged in court. The relative-responsibility clause placing more of the burden of support upon the recipients' parents or children proved unpopular and was watered down by subsequent legislation. Finally, the entire focus of the act was mainly upon reducing the costs of the program regardless of the needs of the recipients. Reagan's description of the latter was as follows: "Most of these are people who either through lack of basic education or lack of any kind of motivation, lack of any job skill, or maybe just because they don't want to work—these are the welfare recipients."[4] This represents an almost classic instance of a political style known as "blaming the victim" since it fails to recognize that approximately three-fourths of the recipients were aged, blind, or disabled and that the great preponderance of the remainder were children in one-parent households whose average grant per child (under the AFDC program) was $800 a year. Since the state was spending about $1,100 per child per year in public education, the adequacy of California's welfare system was doubtful, especially after the Reagan-Moretti "reforms."

The remaining years of the Reagan administration saw repeated reversals of his ideological principles and a sustained triumph of his image. Inflation and the economic upturn brought state budget increases—from $6.8 billion in fiscal year 1971-1972 to $7.9 billion in 1972-1973 to $9.3 billion in 1973-

1974—and simultaneous demands for property tax relief at the local level which could only be financed by increases in state taxes. This process had actually begun in 1968 when the Los Angeles County assessor, Philip Watson, placed an initiative proposal on the ballot to reduce local property taxes drastically, a proposal that was defeated when the state legislature successfully countered with a proposal to grant a statewide property tax reduction of $70 per homeowner. In 1971 the legislature passed similar legislation for elderly homeowners threatened with the loss of their homes through large tax increases, and in the following year Watson succeeded again in qualifying a large property tax reduction initiative. Ironically, both Reagan and Democratic leaders in the legislature strongly opposed this initiative and promised the electorate a tax reform law to expand greatly property tax relief through homeowners' exemptions on their state income taxes if the Watson initiative were defeated. This worked, and after the 1972 election the legislature passed the Reagan-Moretti tax bill, which raised sales taxes to six percent and bank and corporation taxes by 1.4 percent. These taxes proved more than sufficient to finance increased homeowners' exemptions, tax relief for renters, business inventory tax reductions, and increased state outlays for schools, welfare, and county open spaces, and in later years they would generate huge treasury surpluses for the succeeding administration.

Perhaps fearful of a widening gap between his fiscal record and his economizing reputation, Governor Reagan embarked on a major effort in image-renovation in 1973. This was his sponsorship of Proposition One to be decided in a special election in November. The initiative measure was designed to do by constitutional fiat what Reagan had found impossible to do by legislative means. The constitutional amendment would supposedly prohibit the legislature from raising taxes beyond a fixed percentage of the total personal income of the state's taxpayers. The formula devised for doing this was exceedingly complex and there was considerable doubt as to whether or how it could be applied uniformly. Opponents led by Robert Moretti charged that the measure would shift the burden for many necessary state services to local governmental units with property taxpayers paying a disproportionate share. The governor and his advisers mounted a well-planned, well-financed (they outspent their opponents by about 5 to 1) campaign which at first seemed irresistible since it held out the appealing lure of tax reduction and catered to the growing public animus against big government, big spenders, and welfare "cheats." Gradually sentiment shifted against it, however, especially because of the measure's complexity and ambiguity, and when on election eve Reagan himself admitted that he did not understand it and asked the people to vote for it anyway, he probably contributed materially to its defeat. It lost by more than 300,000 votes. Reagan then took a trip out of the country and while he was gone he suffered another fiscal reverse. In order to receive federal matching funds for aid to the aged, blind, and disabled, the state was required to raise its basic grants to these recipients. Reagan had done so by administrative decree and by very minimal amounts—from $212 per month for all three categories to $221 for the aged and disabled and $237 for the blind. A federal court ruled, however, that this could only be done by legislative action, and since the absent governor had no bill to offer, the lieutenant governor had to sign into law the bill passed by the legislature or forfeit several hundred million dollars in federal funds. The bill passed was drawn up by John Burton, a liberal assemblyman and later congressman from San Francisco, and it raised benefits much higher than Reagan helplessly preferred—to $235 and $265 respectively.

The year 1974, Reagan's last year in office, was an ambiguous and anticlimactic one for the governor. His conservative image was still intact as his defeat on Proposition One made him look like one who had at least fought the good fight for fiscal restraint, and few noticed that his $10.1 billion budget that year was more than double that when he had first taken office. He had also compiled a fairly creditable record in the environmental field, having signed stringent legislation on air and water quality control and for the requirement of environmental impact reports on public works projects. His personal election victories, while exhilarating, had done little to advance the electoral fortunes of the Republican party, however, for the Democrats controlled both houses of the legislature for six of his eight years in office. His attempts to redress the balance by fighting the Democrats on the reapportionment issue also failed, for his vetoes of their apportionment bills simply caused the state supreme court to draw the new map of legislative and congressional districts after the 1970 census, and this new redistricting plan proved no more advantageous to the Republicans than the old one had been. The election of 1974 was a Republican debacle. Edmund G. Brown, Jr., defeated the moderate Houston Flournoy for governor, and the Democrats carried every other state constitutional office except that of the attorney general. They widened their lead on the congressional delegation (28 to 15) and gained nearly commanding control of the state legislature— 24 to 15 with one vacancy in the senate, and 54 to 25 with one vacancy in the assembly. Whatever contributions Ronald Reagan had made to California politics, revitalizing the Republican party was not one of them.

Still, in 1975 his reputation as a great conservative had never been higher. After leaving the governorship he stepped up his media campaign to keep it that way. In addition to personal speaking tours and television speeches, he wrote a syndicated newspaper column and spoke on a regularly scheduled series of radio broadcasts. The huge growth of his nationwide following reflected his continuing mastery of the mass media and the latter demonstrated again their awesome power to inflict upon the masses a kind of historical amnesia about recent events. Reagan in 1976 came very close to capturing the Republican presidential nomination from White House incumbent Gerald Ford, and other presidential candidates today are feeling his discomforting presence as well.

CHAPTER SIX

Jerry Brown and the "New Spirit"

THE GOVERNORSHIP OF Edmund G. Brown, Jr., blends in strange ways the unique and the familiar. The only son of "Pat" Brown, he early adopted the name of "Jerry" (his middle name is Gerald) to distinguish himself from his famous father. In many ways he has struggled ever since to free himself from his father's influence while capitalizing upon their relationship at the same time. The Brown name was a priceless advantage at the start of his political career, and his father's connections have proven continually useful for fundraising and other purposes. These connections, however, also aroused expectations that he would govern the state in his father's liberal-pragmatic way, which in turn have probably heightened the governor's determination to be different, a determination in which sometimes he has been spectacularly successful.

In his adolescence he seemed bent on abjuring political life altogether when he entered a Jesuit seminary to prepare for the priesthood. After nearly four years there he withdrew, however, and with the aid of his father who cut through the red tape in the admissions office, he enrolled immediately at the University of California, Berkeley, graduating in 1961. Again with his father's assistance, he received a scholarship to the Yale University Law School, from which he graduated in 1964, and after five years of rather desultory law practice in San Francisco and Los Angeles, he plunged into a political career.

His first run for office was a 1969 campaign for a seat on the newly created Los Angeles Junior College Board. Running against a total of 132 largely unknown candidates for seven seats, he openly campaigned on his father's name and easily won the largest number of votes in both the primary and general elections. His service on the board was brief, undistinguished, and often absentee, but it gave him a political base for his next bid for office, the secretaryship of state in 1970. This was also successful, as the magic of the Brown name proved overwhelming in the primary race against state Senator Hugh Burns, an old-time rival as well as ally of Pat Brown's, and against a little known Republican, James Flournoy (not to be confused with State Controller Houston Flournoy), in the fall election.

As secretary of state, Jerry Brown first began to establish a political identity separate from that of "the Old Man's son." Although the office of secretary of state had usually been regarded as a rather dull administrative sinecure, he seized upon its power to enforce the campaign disclosure laws and dramatically announce his intention to prosecute a number of corporations and 134 candidates (mostly Republicans) for noncompliance. Brown also benefited from the national Watergate scandal when his office discovered that President Richard Nixon's attorney had illegally backdated a notarized document giving away Nixon's vice presidential papers in order to get an unauthorized income-tax deducation. Even more advantageously, Brown helped to sponsor a 1974 Fair Political Practices initiative which placed rigid controls on campaign funding and required much more thorough disclosures of financial assets and spending by both officeholders and lobbyists. Although the act was later partly invalidated by the courts, it gave Brown an image of purity which was not shared by most other politicians during the Watergate era. All of Brown's actions, furthermore, were accompanied by barrages of publicity which were astutely managed by his closest adviser, Thomas Quinn, a former news service executive who taught Brown how to become the master of the media that he has since proved to be.

It was a foregone conclusion that Brown would run for governor in 1974. His dramatic stewardship as secretary of state and his sponsorship of the political reform initiative gave him an advantage over his Democratic opponents in the primary. They were worthy antagonists, especially Mayor Joseph Alioto of San Francisco and Assembly Speaker Robert Moretti, but he easily defeated them (38 percent of the vote compared to their 19 percent and 17 percent respectively). With all Republicans smitten by the Watergate backlash, he seemed a shoo-in in the general election. Brown accordingly conducted a deliberately dull campaign in which he talked vaguely of bringing a "new spirit" to Sacramento and avoided discussing basic issues (especially in statewide televised debates) with the Republican candidate, Houston Flournoy. This proved to be a dangerous miscalculation, for Flournoy gained dramatically in the opinion polls. When the election was held Brown defeated him by less than a three-percent margin. If Brown was going to bring a new spirit to California government, he would be doing so with something less than an overwhelming popular mandate.

Within a year, however, Jerry Brown transformed himself into one of the most admired and popular figures in public life and was given highly favorable ratings in the opinion polls by more than eighty percent of the populace. Unlike his father, who was also popular during his first year in office, he did not gain public approbation by securing the passage of a mass of major legislation. In fact only one outstanding legislative enactment was passed in 1975 with the governor's personal sponsorship. This was the path-breaking Agricultural Labor Relations Act, which at long last brought government-sponsored collective bargaining procedures to farm laborers in the state, and was a triumph for the charismatic César Chávez, head of the United Farm Workers, as well as for Jerry Brown. Although this was a landmark achievement for which the governor deserves enduring recognition for the dominant role he played in its passage, it can hardly account for the massive popular adulation he received. What does account for it?

The answer to this question may lie in the profound, silent, revolution that has taken place in contemporary California politics. This is mainly a television revolution, which Ronald Reagan first exploited, and which Brown has come to understand better than any other modern politician. In mastering this medium of communication for political purposes, what one does is far less important than what one is or what one appears to be. Projecting a captivating image of oneself is more important than compiling a list of legislative achievements, and Brown proved adept at giving the viewer-voter a good show. "First there was Reagan, the entertainer turned politician, and now there was Jerry, the politician turned entertainer," said James Lorenz, one of Brown's disgruntled former associates.[1] Realizing that a credible public protagonist needs a scapegoat to attack, Lorenz also asserts that "in early February 1975, Jerry hit upon a solution. He would scapegoat the government."[2] Sensitive to the public's anti-governmental mood in the post-Vietnam, post-Watergate era, he charged that government could not solve all (or any) of society's hardest problems, that people should "lower their expectations" of what could be achieved and recognize that the state and nation were entering an "era of limits." To the jaded public's immense amusement he began attacking governmental bureaucracy by making sudden appearances at agency meetings and asking pointed questions about their functions and effectiveness. Probably his most spectacular effort of this sort was his performance before the California Welfare Directors Association where he stacked 34 volumes of federal and state welfare laws, containing mainly "mishmash," he said, alongside of a copy of the Old Testament, which he lauded for its clarity and conciseness. While this and other "happenings" of a similar sort brought no perceptible improvements in governmental policies, they dramatized his disenchantment with traditional governmental processes and doubtless struck a responsive chord with the general public.

To further the perceived difference between himself and the typical bureaucrat and politician, he cultivated a highly individual life-style and saw to it that it also was widely publicized. Announcing that he would not live in the newly constructed governor's mansion, he rented a modest apartment near the Capitol grounds. Instead of a pretentious Cadillac for his personal transportation he chose a modest Plymouth sedan. On official as well as personal trips he flew tourist class, and his inexpensive mode of living was echoed by an unorthodox personal philosophy which he ceaselessly articulated in the slogan "Small Is Beautiful." Based on a book of the same name by a

British economist, E. F. Schumacher, the theory asserts that the viability of an economic system should be judged not on the basis of how much it produces but on how little it produces and still takes care of society's basic needs. Designed to discourage excessive consumption rather than to encourage it, as capitalism allegedly does, the philosophy is also well suited to protecting the environment and conserving natural resources, both very popular appeals at the time. The philosophy was also attractive to many because it was labeled "Buddhist economics," and when Brown let it be known that he was a practitioner of contemplation, often at San Francisco's Zen Center, he seemed additionally fascinating to an already intrigued general public.

In at least two other ways Brown enhanced his image before the electorate. One was his stance on environmental issues. From the first his speeches were full of ecology rhetoric, and he angered businessmen by attacking their "cowboy ethic" whereby they allegedly sought only to take things out of the environment without putting anything back, and angered them still more by his sustained opposition to the building of nuclear power plants in the state. Instead he endorsed alternate energy sources and established an Office of Appropriate Technology to explore possibilities in this and related areas. Later he sponsored a save-the-whales celebration and appointed his close associate Tom Quinn chairman of the Air Resources Board, and Quinn cracked down on automotive and other industries for violations of air quality standards.

His appointments, like that of Quinn, were the other main means of ingratiating himself with the public. Commenting in early 1975 about his appointments policy he said, "Foremost, I don't have a bunch of businessmen." Instead he prided himself on the "sensitive and committed human beings" who made up his official "family" in the state house (he was a bachelor and as he was somewhat estranged from his parents, it was the only real family he had), and most of them were distinctly nonestablishment types. Mainly young attorneys, they came largely from backgrounds in public-interest law, public defenders' offices, and the American Civil Liberties Union. In his other appointments he became genuinely famous for his selections from the ranks of racial minorities and women. Although scores could be named, probably the most important were: Mario Obledo, of

Mexican ancestry, named secretary of health and welfare; Wiley Manuel, a black superior court judge appointed associate justice of the state supreme court; and Rose Elizabeth Bird, chosen to be the first female chief justice of the state supreme court. Brown also backed the passage of a law to increase the number of general-public members appointed to various state licensing commissions, and although this aroused opposition from business and professional groups, it was enthusiastically supported by the lay public.

Thus far, despite the hoopla and fanfare, the Brown record was not a radical departure from liberal expectations and conservative fears. When he came to fiscal matters, however, the hard core of any administration's program, Brown sent his liberal supporters into a state of shock from which they have not yet recovered. Shrewdly sensing that public enthusiasm for his antigovernment, "small-is-beautiful," "era-of-limits" rhetoric reflected an even more deep-seated mass antipathy toward taxing and spending policies, Brown early announced and constantly repeated that there would be no general tax increases during his term. His first budget, calling for total expenditures of $11.3 billion, was less than five percent higher than the previous year's total appropriations, an increase that was smaller than the annual rate of inflation. Although the legislature would manage, as usual, to increase total spending by a few hundreds of millions of dollars, the basic legislative-executive deadlock over dollars would remain, and Governor Brown's fiscal role has been mainly to perpetuate that of Governor Reagan rather than to repudiate it. Given the fact that Brown's 1974 campaign speeches were full of attacks on "recycled Reaganism," it is not surprising that many Republicans (including Reagan) have become unexpectedly jubilant over Brown's performance nor that many liberals view it with a growing sense of betrayal.

It is, of course, more than a debate over money that divides Brown from his critics. At issue is the basic question of the role of government in modern society. The liberal-pragmatic tradition has been that social problems arise and that government studies them and seeks to resolve them, or reduce their seriousness, usually by spending money. Brown attacked this when submitting his first budget as "the dollar chasing a problem" approach. Unfortunately he neglected to mention what he would substitute for dollars when pursuing a problem, and increasingly his critics have come to suspect that the answer is rhetoric, or that he would refuse to chase it at all. The most dramatic instance of this was the in-house quarrel over a jobs program. Unemployment, especially among ghetto youth, is an extremely serious problem in California where the jobless rate is higher than in the nation at large. Brown appointed James Lorenz, a former poverty lawyer, to develop a jobs program, but Lorenz soon began to complain that the governor seemed little interested in his proposals. When the *Los Angeles Times* attacked the administration for inaction, Brown allegedly told his subordinates, "I'll show them. I'll do something. . . . We'll have a flurry of activity."[3] He and Quinn then announced the inauguration of a billion-dollar water and sewer project designed to create 37,000 jobs and improve water quality at the same time. Business, labor, and environmental groups, such as the Sierra Club, all enthusiastically applauded the program, and it was only later discovered that it was financed by the federal government after the U.S. Supreme Court forced the release of funds that had been appropriated several years earlier but had been illegally impounded by President Nixon.

Federal funding of the program was doubly ironic because the governor had been consistently attacking the federal government for its bureaucratic hampering of state government's efforts to deal with such problems. Attacking federal grant-in-aid policies as "too complicated" and as embodying "phony money" schemes, he turned down some $64 million from Washington for job programs, according to Lorenz. When the latter drew up a detailed proposal for a jobs program that enlisted the aid of many private local groups and linked employment projects with environmental protection efforts, the proposal fell into the hands of a conservative newspaper, the *Oakland Tribune,* which labeled it "Brown's Secret Plan for Worker State." Embarrassed by the adverse publicity charging him with "socialist" inclinations, Brown repudiated the proposal and called for Lorenz's resignation; when Lorenz refused, he fired him in July 1975. The jobs program has been in limbo ever since, and the governor has taken to arguing that unemployment is a "national" problem and presumably solvable only through action by the federal government. How federal actions could pass his tests of not being "too complicated" or employing "phony money" policies has not been made clear.

The governor encountered similar difficulties in the Health and Welfare Agency. A huge bureaucracy, and admittedly an administrative monstrosity created by a pseudo-reorganization plan of Governor Reagan, the agency was also beset by two scandals. One was in the Medi-Cal program, which had sought to save money by inducing (and pressuring) recipients to join "prepaid" medical organizations which would hopefully provide better quality care at a lower cost to the state. They did neither, and some organizations were outright "rackets." The other scandal was in the Department of Mental Health, which had never recovered fully from Reagan's budget cuts. When Brown also vetoed legislative efforts to increase hospital staffing, the situation again deteriorated. It was revealed in 1976 that 139 patient deaths had occurred in the preceding two years and many could be attributed, at least in part, to shortages in hospital staffs. Neither of these problems has been solved to any appreciable extent, for there is little doubt that solving them would involve large budget increases which Brown wished to avoid. On the other hand, the governor capably preserved a public image of himself as a humane executive genuinely concerned over the plight of the suffering by making dramatic visits to state hospitals and announcing before the television cameras that he was urging the legislature to pass emergency appropriations. He could not do much by refusing to chase problems with dollars, but he could appear to be doing a great deal.

Appearances counted for very much in 1976 because the governor decided to run for president that year. Although he came late to the race, too late to stop Jimmy Carter as it turned out, he won in a number of state primaries and acquired an enthusiastic, even hysterical, out-of-state following who hailed him as a new phenomenon and a refreshing contrast to the old-style "politicians" in the public arena. Ironically, in Maryland, the first and most important state where he defeated Carter, he did so in part by behaving very much like a traditional politician. He sought and secured the support of a notorious Democratic political machine, and he outspent the Carter forces in a very effective campaign blitz. He then unsurprisingly defeated Carter in nearby Nevada, where his influence was strong, lost in Oregon (he ran a respectable third with a write-in candidacy, however), and campaigned successfully for uncommitted slates in Rhode Island and New Jersey. These two primaries were nominal defeats for Carter but not real victories for Brown. (The New Jersey uncommitted delegation supported Hubert Humphrey and in Rhode Island the delegates were fragmented into three groups.)

Finally, in California Brown routed Carter by getting 59 percent of the vote to Carter's 20 percent. Whatever his standing nationally Brown struck a magic formula with the voters in his home state. Presenting himself as a moderate he took credit for such conservative achievements as the "low" budget (appropriations rose to about $13 billion in 1976 from $11.36 billion in 1975), mandatory sentences for criminals, and small pay increases ($70 per month regardless of position) for state empoyees. This was balanced by his endorsement of such liberal enactments as the Agricultural Labor Relations Act, the closing of some business tax loopholes, a public housing program for low-income families, the establishment of "lifeline" utility rates, and a package of nuclear safety laws designed to defeat a much more radical initiative measure dealing with this subject. After the primary he also personally backed, unlike his stance on a number of the above issues, a bill to protect the California coastline in line with an initiative measure recently passed. While such appeals no doubt contributed to his presidential primary victory, they were all for nought. Carter had already won control of the Democratic convention, and although Brown, perhaps naïvely, refused to concede to the very end, he returned home with empty hands but possibly with an enhanced image.

He also probably returned with an unquenchable thirst for the presidency and an irresistible urge to try again. Most of his policies since then, which often appear wildly inconsistent and irrational, seem less so when calculated against the likelihood of a presidential nomination in 1980 or 1984. Elected by a largely liberal constituency, he was quick to sense a shift in public opinion to a more conservative mood, and he has proved adept in appealing to this conservative sentiment while retaining much liberal support as well. As a liberal on personal freedoms he willingly signed laws relaxing restrictions on sexual activities between consenting adults and lightening penalties on marijuana possession. Sensitive to charges of being soft on crime and immorality, on the other hand, he signed legislation for stiffer and mandatory penalties for felons committing violent crimes, and when a female state official in the Department of Health wrote a private but allegedly "obscene" letter on official stationery he sought unsuccessfully to fire her. Liberal supporters were once again placated when he announced in advance that he would veto any bill prescribing the death penalty and kept his promise in 1977. Conservatives and hard-liners were mollified, however, when he made no attempt to prevent his veto from being overridden, which it was, and the death penalty question immediately faded as a campaign issue.

More pronounced were Brown's shifts on issues regarding business and the environment. At first Brown's "small is beautiful," "era of limits" slogans seemed hostile to business and business expansion. David Packard, an industrial magnate and Republican fund raiser, asked publicly in 1975 whether business could get a fair hearing from the poverty lawyers and their ilk who surrounded Brown. Later in the year the Fantus Company, a subsidiary of the *Wall Street Journal,* issued a report listing California third from last among all states in providing a "probusiness climate." In early 1977 the Dow Chemical Company announced that it was abandoning plans to locate a large manufacturing plant in the state because of excessive bureaucratic and environmental roadblocks thrown up by the state government. The would-be future president was not unaware of the liabilities of being tagged as antibusiness in a capitalist country. Soon he began talking of an "era of possibilities" rather than one of limits and he declared that jobs came before the environment on his list of priorities. He made a trip to Japan attempting to induce that nation to locate an auto assembly plant in the state, and with appropriate fanfare he announced the launching of a "California Means Business" campaign. Aware of the crucial importance of the aerospace industry in California's economy, Brown held a 1977 space symposium in Los Angeles to glorify the launching of the space shuttle, and in January 1978 he proposed that the legislature appropriate some six million dollars for the launching of the first state-owned communications satellite and for the establishment of a space institute at the University of California.

Brown's appointments also began to reflect a probusiness stance, and it began to appear that he might surround himself with "a bunch of businessmen" after all. Business executives Alan Rothenberg and Richard Silberman both served stints as secretary of business and transportation, and Silberman later moved up to the all-important position of state director of finance. Russell ("Rusty") Schweikart serves the governor as science and technology assistant, thereby making California the first state to have an astronaut-in-residence, presumably to preside over the now defunct state satellite program. Richard Rominger, a farmer and strong supporter of agribusiness, has been appointed director of the Department of Food and Agriculture, and Brown has been zealous in his efforts to gain support among the growers in the state who resented his backing of the Agricultural Labor Relations Act. He has attempted to appoint members to the Agricultural Labor Relations Board who are more sympathetic to the growers' viewpoint, and he has reversed himself on the 160-acre limitation clause to the growers' benefit.

To the dismay of many environmentalists, Brown allowed Tom Quinn to negotiate for the installation of both an Alaskan oil terminal and a liquid natural gas storage facility in southern California. (The oil terminal and pipeline project has now been abandoned, however.) Others applaud the safety and clean air provisions in the contracts secured by Quinn, and all antinuclear folk have applauded the governor's consistent stand against new nuclear power generating plants in the state and his endorsement of solar energy and other alternative power sources. Although such endorsements might appear more symbol than substance, they seem to make it difficult for many environmental liberals to desert the governor despite his seeming desertion of their cause in many instances. His strategy of retaining his liberal backing while picking up conservative support appears to be working well.

On one issue, however, Brown made a miscalculation serious enough to have smashed his well-laid plans to bits. Ironically, it was the issue that he thought he understood best and regarding which he had striven most strenuously to protect himself from harm. It was the fiscal issue. Operating on the assumption that the thing most to be avoided was a tax increase, Brown had consistently fought to keep spending down so that no new taxes would be necessary. His tight $14.3 billion budget of 1977–1978 was designed to limit spending for state services in order to allocate several billion dollars to local school districts in order to implement the state supreme court's 1971 decision in *Serrano v. Priest. Serrano* required the state to equalize funding of public education and reduce the inequalities between poor and wealthy districts. The passing of Brown's school funding law, although still under challenge in the courts, was a significant achievement. It did not deplete a large and growing state treasury surplus, however, and Brown underestimated the enormous efficiency of the Reagan-Moretti tax laws in generating unexpectedly high revenues. Inflation played a major role, of course, because it put state income taxpayers into higher tax brackets even though their real incomes had not increased. Republicans demanded that income taxes be "indexed" (graduating them according to the consumer price index rather than mere dollar amounts of income), but Brown opposed this in 1977 fearing that the reduction in revenue would deplete the treasury surplus and raise the grim specter of a tax increase in 1978 when he would be running for reelection. (A limited indexing law was passed in 1979.)

Such trepidation could hardly have been more unfounded. The Sacramento money machine was rapidly accelerating the accumulation of a treasury surplus which reached well over $5 billion by the end of the year. With the income tax relief hatch closed, the voters' demands for tax reduction came to focus on another tax which they resented even more—the property tax. As previously noted, initiative efforts to reduce property taxes by fixing them at one percent of true market value had been made three times since 1968, but the legislature had defeated them at the polls by passing piecemeal property tax relief measures and arguing that the state could not afford further reductions. The huge treasury surpluses now made such arguments seem laughable, and when Brown failed to induce the legislature to pass a "circuit breaker" tax relief law (granting proportionately more property tax relief to persons with lower incomes) in 1977, the ground was prepared for a new property tax initiative which qualified for the 1978 ballot with an astounding 1.2 million signatures. This was the famous Proposition 13, also known as the Jarvis-Gann amendment.

Jarvis-Gann was an exercise in "radical conservatism." Although it was supported by masses of middle- and lower-income homeowners, it provided many more benefits to the affluent than to the deprived. By fixing property taxes at no more than one percent of true market value, it provided progressively more tax savings to those with the more valuable properties, and since it applied uniformly to business property as well as residences, it brought much more in tax savings to commercial and industrial proprietors than to homeowners. It was especially advantageous to apartment-house owners, who would enjoy lower taxes but could still raise rents, and disadvantageous to renters for the same reasons. Governor Brown, probably thinking that public opinion would turn against it when these inequities became generally known, publicly labeled the measure a "rip-off" and resorted to the previously tried-and-true strategy to defeat it. He induced the legislature to pass a less sweeping property tax-relief amendment and referred it to the voters in oposition to Proposition 13. This was the "Behr bill" which would provide about $1.4 billion in tax relief (Jarvis-Gann would provide an estimated $7 billion) and confine the tax limitation solely to residential properties. For perhaps the first time, however, the governor's sensitive political antenna sent him the wrong signals, and in the primary election of 1978 in which he was easily renominated (he had no significant opposition in the Democratic party), Proposition 13 also passed by a margin so overwhelming that it made his uncontested victory look insignificant by comparison.

Brown was seemingly in deep political trouble in his reelection campaign of 1978. Not only had he been on the "wrong side" of what proved to be an overwhelmingly popular measure, but his opponent for governor, Attorney General Evelle Younger, had endorsed Proposition 13 and was a seasoned politician who had never lost an election. In one of the most dazzling displays of political footwork in California history, however, Brown soon stole the advantage away from his opponent and converted the issue to his own use. On election night when the results of the Proposition 13 vote were in, he began talking about implementing the measure "in a humane way" and never again said a bad word about it. While Younger took a leisurely vacation in Hawaii, Brown seized the initiative by meeting with the legislature to work out the procedures whereby the some seven billion dollars of treasury surpluses were allocated to local governmental units to offset the drastic fall-off in revenues due to curtailment of the property tax. He immediately declared a hiring freeze on state employees and called on the legislature to deny pay increases to them as well as to public assistance recipients. Finally, he appointed a special commission headed by the respected former legislative analyst, Alan Post, to conduct a study of state governmental costs and their possibilities of reduction. All of this was accompanied by a barrage of economizing rhetoric and television exposure designed to project an image of the governor as a leading proponent of Proposition 13 and to make the public forget that he had ever opposed it. While conservatives cheered (Howard Jarvis endorsed Brown as well as Younger!), liberals jeered, and cynics sneered about the "Jarvis-Brown Amendment," Brown gained massive public support and overwhelmed his opponent in the fall election by about the same margin of votes by which Proposition 13 had passed in the primary. It was a display of political virtuosity, if nothing else, the likes of which the state had seldom seen.

Since the opening of the 1979 legislative session Governor Brown has sought to persuade the legislature, the public, and perhaps himself, that his newfound conservative persuasion was not a mere election campaign conversion. His proposed $21 billion budget was no higher than the previous one if the new allocations to local governments were again added in, and for the first time he aroused the direct opposition of Assembly Speaker Leo McCarthy to his penny-pinching principles. McCarthy insisted that welfare recipients be granted catch-up increases of 15.7 percent, as required by law, while Brown proposed a six percent increase. McCarthy argued that his proposal would raise AFDC grants by only an average of $28 monthly to a total of about $322 per month (the aged and disabled would receive $354 and the blind $397), still only enough for bare survival. But Brown pointed to a state savings of nearly $300 million by adopting the six percent figure and feared that state employees would also demand more than a six percent raise if welfare grantees received more. Although this argument seemed in conflict with the governor's earlier statements that when economizing or "belt tightening" in government "those with the biggest belts ought to make the biggest sacrifices and tighten them up the most," it probably rang true to the average citizen.[4] The issue soon became obscured, however, because of massive publicity given to a more sensational gubernatorial proposal.

In his first message to the 1979 legislature Brown astounded that body by calling for an amendment to the United States Constitution requiring an annually balanced federal budget. Furthermore, he requested the legislature to pass a resolution to that effect and to petition Congress to summon a national constitutional convention to approve the amendment rather than to submit it to the states for approval as had been the procedure for every other constitutional amendment. Brown's procedure is considered perilous by many constitutional scholars who fear that a convention might produce dangerous changes in the Constitution, and by liberals who are incensed that Brown would support such a risky venture for a highly conservative cause. A national movement for such a convention and for such an amendment was already under way, and Brown has enthusiastically endorsed it as the only way to ensure fiscal "sanity" in Washington, D.C., and to forestall the "bankruptcy" of government already threatened by deficit spending and runaway inflation. The California legislature, again led by McCarthy, defeated the proposal (although McCarthy endorsed a call for a balanced federal budget), and the state's congressional delegation has also rebuffed him. Members of the latter point out that Brown calls for federal funds for various state programs at the same time that he demands that the federal government reduce its expenditures and balance its budget. If Brown and other state governors, they assert, were willing to reject federal funds and revenue-sharing grants, the federal government could balance its budget without a constitutional amendment. Such arguments may nor may not prove to be as persuasive to voters as they are to officeholders, and Brown's budget-balancing rhetoric seems thus far very popular and may put him into a strong position to challenge President Jimmy Carter for the presidential nomination in 1980. (Brown announced his candidacy in November 1979.)

In July 1979, however, Jerry Brown learned that playing presidential and gubernatorial politics at the same time is a tricky business. State legislators were nearly unanimous in their opposition to his presidential ambitions—Republicans because he would threaten Ronald Reagan's chances for the office, and Democrats because if he gained the White House he would necessarily relinquish the state house to the Republican lieutenant governor Mike Curb. As a result the legislature turned on Brown with an unprecedented three humiliating veto overrides in less than three weeks. One was on a relatively innocuous measure prohibiting banks from selling insurance but the other two defeated his efforts to eliminate or curtail salary increases for state employees, the main feature of his post–Proposition 13 economy drive. Since he had already capitulated to Speaker McCarthy on increased welfare payments, and since he chose not to risk further overrides by refraining from vetoing any appropriations in the legislature's massive $4.85 billion "bailout" bill for local governments, his image as economizer extraordinary became somewhat tarnished.

Likewise his efforts to rebuild his bridges to the political left suffered at least a partial legislative checkmate. His closest political associates in this area were the widely known left-wing activists actress Jane Fonda and her husband Tom Hayden. He appointed Hayden to two state commissions and nominated Fonda to the California Arts Council, but he aroused the greatest controversy when he named a highly controversial left-wing associate of theirs, Edison Miller, as interim county supervisor in highly conservative Orange County. Legislators could not block the latter appointment since it did not require legislative confirmation, but they did refuse to confirm Fonda's nomination to the Arts Council. As a result Brown's ability to "deliver the goods" to the liberal-left was rendered questionable.

If Brown's rapid reversals of policy and position can be understood in light of his ultimate political objectives, they nevertheless make his administration difficult to categorize. While the other governors studied can be classified fairly clearly as liberal or conservative, ideological or pragmatic, Jerry Brown's ideological gymnastics and political flip-flops give the student a

severe case of classificatory indigestion. While his tactics can be
rated as pragmatic in the sense that they are directed toward
gaining and holding office, philosophically they often seem to
reflect no deep-seated principles whatsoever (unless a burning
conviction of the desirability of Jerry Brown being president
can be called a principle). "You watch," he allegedly once told
an associate, "I'm going to move right and left at the same
time."[5] Another associate, remarking on one of his notorious
reversals of position, reportedly said, "It's so typical. Jerry has a
whim of iron." When asked if she meant will of iron, she said,
"No, no. A whim of iron. He changes his mind all of the time,
but he does it so resolutely."[6] Still another associate calls Brown
an "eclectic pragmatist,"[7] but one wonders if his admitted eclec-
ticism indicates an open mind or one that is simply too porous
to hold a conviction. Some unfairly blame his Jesuit training for
his alleged insincerity, but the Jesuit order has worked long and
strenuously to overcome their once widespread reputation of
unprincipled deviousness in pursuit of fixed ends and as origina-
tors of the amoral aphorism that ends justify means. Still,
Brown's antics ironically often seem perfectly suited to revive
this unflattering image. One of his life-long friends and fellow
seminarian and fellow dropout from seminary training described
their experiences on the debate team of the Jesuit high school
they attended: "We were set up even then for this great Jesu-
itical thinking, argue either side of any subject at any time. And
no matter what the debate topic was, no matter which side we
were on, he [Brown] would always end up saying, 'What we
need is a flexible plan for an ever-changing world.' That's a great
quote, 'a flexible plan for an ever-changing world.' And I'll tell
you, by God, he's got a flexible plan."[8]

By God, if he hasn't!

NOTES

CHAPTER ONE

1. Stephens's election victory in 1918 was somewhat of a "fluke," however, because he had no opponent in the fall election due to the curious functioning of the famous crossfiling law then in effect. H. Brett Melendy, "California's Cross-Filing Nightmare: The 1918 Gubernatorial Election," *Pacific Historical Review,* XXXII (August, 1964), 317–330.

2. This amendment outlawed the manufacture, sale, or transportation of intoxicating beverages throughout the U.S.

3. It was declared unconstitutional by the U.S. Supreme Court in 1969.

4. The Democratic party had become so weak by this time that California had become practically a one-party state. Therefore the key electoral canvass was now the Republican primary, not the general election.

5. Hiram Johnson, running for reelection as U.S. senator, played an ironic nonrole in the campaign by failing to endorse Stephens. Although Johnson won by a margin of three times the number of votes which Stephens needed to win, Johnson refused to enable his old enemy to ride into office on his political coat-tails.

6. California's population grew from 3.4 million to about 5.7 million between 1920 and 1930, an increase of about 63 percent.

7. Ironically Richardson's defeat was partly due to the opposition of one of California's biggest businesses, the Bank of Italy, soon to become the Bank of America. Richardson had opposed the corporation's branch banking policies, and when Young promised it "fair treatment," the bank directed its considerable influence to Young's support. Russell M. Posner, "The Bank of Italy and the 1926 Campaign in California," *California Historical Society Quarterly,* XXXVII (September 1958), 267–275, and (December 1958), 347–358.

CHAPTER TWO

1. The federal plan was an initiative constitutional amendment which stipulated that no county could have more than one state senator and

that no more than three counties could be merged into one senatorial district. This discriminated flagrantly against populous counties, such as Los Angeles, in favor of sparsely populated rural ones, such as Alpine, Mono, and Mariposa. Thomas S. Barclay, "Reapportionment in California," *Pacific Historical Review*, V (June 1936), 93–129.

2. Max Stern in San Francisco *News*, November 2, 1934, quoted in Jackson K. Putnam, *Old-Age Politics in California* (Stanford, 1970), p. 38.

3. This was a deft touch since Johnson had supported FDR in 1932 and was in the process of being rewarded by the Democrats who mounted only a token campaign against him. This enabled Johnson to crossfile successfully on the Democratic ticket and thus become the first U.S. senator in history to win election as the candidate of both major parties. In 1940 he repeated this triumph and this time over FDR's opposition, as Johnson by this time had broken with the New Deal over foreign-policy matters.

4. Carey McWilliams, *California: The Great Exception* (Santa Barbara and Salt Lake City: Peregrine Smith, 1976), pp. 207–213.

5. Arthur H. Samish and Bob Thomas, *The Secret Boss of California: The Life and High Times of Art Samish* (New York: Crown Publishers, 1971), pp. 44–45, 71.

6. Olson apparently was not merely an occasional snooper. When his successor Earl Warren took over the governorship, he found that all of the executive offices had been "bugged" with listening and recording devices. The recordings had all been removed, however, along with all of the previous governor's "personal" files. Earl Warren, *The Memoirs of Earl Warren* (Garden City, N.Y.: Doubleday, 1971), 168–169.

CHAPTER THREE

1. Richard B. Harvey, *Earl Warren, Governor of California* (Jericho, N.Y.: Exposition Press, 1969), pp. 97–98; Leo Katcher, *Earl Warren: A Political Biography* (New York: McGraw-Hill, 1967), p. 177.

2. "Right-to-work" laws were designed to put an end to the "union shop" system whereby a worker would be required to join the union recognized by his fellow employees as their bargaining agent after he had hired on as an employee. Featherbedding means union rules requiring more workers than necessary for a given job or requiring more hours than necessary to complete it.

3. "Hot cargo" refers to goods produced by strikebreakers or from a source involved in a labor dispute. Unions often refused to handle

such good and the hot cargo bill prohibited such a refusal. The apportionment initiative sought to end the "federal plan" in the state which had resulted in undue representation in the state senate of the rural, usually antiunion, interests.

4. Katcher, *Earl Warren*, p. 173.

5. Royce Delmatier et al., *The Rumble of California Politics, 1848–1970* (New York: John Wiley, 1970), p. 314.

6. *Ibid.*, p. 313; Charles R. Titus and Charles R. Nixon, "The 1948 Elections in California," *Western Political Quarterly*, II (March 1949), 97–102.

7. Among Warren's anti-Communist credentials were his opposition to Governor Culbert Olson's pardon of Thomas Mooney and his more outspoken opposition to Olson's commutation of the sentences of the convicted defendants in the *Point Lobos* or "ship murder" case of the 1930s. The latter were Communist party members convicted of the murder of a ship captain in a labor dispute. Warren had been prosecuting attorney in the case and greatly resented their release, partly because of their radicalism and in part because of allegations that they had not received a fair trial.

CHAPTER FOUR

1. The 160-acre limitation was a federal rule that a farmer could get only enough water from a federal water project to irrigate 160 acres. It was designed to encourage small family-type farms and was bitterly opposed by large agribusiness interests.

2. Eugene C. Lee and William Buchanan, "The 1960 Election in California," *Western Political Quarterly*, XIV (March 1961), 310–311.

3. After this election Nixon made his famous announcement that he was quitting politics and castigated the press for picking on him. Six years later he was elected president.

4. The law permitted Republican incumbent officeholders, most of them moderates, to appoint nine members of the state central committee, instead of three as previously, thereby heavily outnumbering the new right-wing members. Totton J. Anderson and Eugene C. Lee, "The 1964 Election in California," *Western Political Quarterly*, XVIII (June 1965, Part 2), 458.

5. Royce Delmatier et al., *The Rumble of California Politics, 1848–1970* (New York: John Wiley, 1970), p. 391.

6. Another party-rending quarrel arose over the state Democratic

chairmanship. When National Committeewoman Carmen Warshaw was defeated for the post by Charles Warren, she blamed Brown for conniving against her and was openly friendly to Reagan and his candidacy for the remainder of the campaign.

CHAPTER FIVE

1. This process had actually begun on a limited scale during the Earl Warren administration, but was much more systematized and expanded by the Short-Doyle Act.

2. Lou Cannon, "The Reagan Years: An Evaluation of the Governor Californians Won't Soon Forget," *California Journal*, November 1974, p. 364. For examples of Reagan's ignorance on various public issues, see Edmund G. Brown and Bill Brown, *Reagan, the Political Chameleon* (New York: Praeger, 1976), pp. 39-43, *passim;* and Frank Kiefer, *I Goofed: The Wise and Curious Sayings of Ronald Reagan ...* (Berkeley: Diablo Press, 1968).

3. Some of the right-wing extremists were not persuaded by Reagan's media campaign and instead began to castigate Reagan as a sell-out and a traitor to true conservatism. For an example, see Kent H. Steffgen, *Here's the Rest of Him* (Reno, Nev.: Foresight Books, 1968). The title derives from Reagan's autobiography entitled *Where's the Rest of Me?* (New York: Duell, Sloan and Pearce, 1965), which was a line Reagan uttered in what probably was his best motion picture, *Kings Row.*

4. "Governor Reagan's Welfare Reform: Plans, Problems and Prospects," *California Journal*, March 1971, pp. 60-63, 78-79.

CHAPTER SIX

1. J. D. Lorenz, *Jerry Brown: The Man on the White Horse* (Boston: Houghton Mifflin, 1978), p. 153.

2. *Ibid., p.* 122.

3. *Ibid.*, p. 67.

4. Robert Pack, *Jerry Brown: The Philosopher Prince* (New York: Stein and Day, 1978), p. 228.

5. Lorenz, p. 123.

6. *Ibid.*, p. 63.

7. Pack, p. 220.

8. *Ibid.*, p. 8.

BIBLIOGRAPHY

General Works

There are five basic California history textbooks, all of which have good coverage of major political events. They are Walton Bean, *California: An Interpretive History* (3rd ed., New York: McGraw-Hill, 1978); Warren A. Beck and David A. Williams, *California: A History of the Golden State* (Garden City, N.Y.: Doubleday, 1972); John W. Caughey, *California: A Remarkable State's Life History* (3rd ed., Englewood Cliffs, N.J.: Prentice-Hall, 1970); Andrew F. Rolle, *California: A History* (Arlington Heights, Ill.: AHM, 1978); and Edward Staniford, *The Pattern of California History* (San Francisco: Canfield, 1975). Excellent specialized works include Royce Delmatier *et al., The Rumble of California Politics, 1848–1970* (New York: John Wiley & Sons, 1970); H. Brett Melendy and Benjamin F. Gilbert, *The Governors of California: Peter H. Burnet to Edmund G. Brown* (Georgetown, Calif.: Talisman Press, 1965); and Michael P. Rogin and John L. Shover, *Political Change in California, 1890–1966* (Westport, Conn.: Greenwood Press, 1970). Two very readable and often informative popular political histories are Gladwyn Hill, *Dancing Bear: An Inside Look at California Politics* (Cleveland: World Publishing Co., 1968); and Herbert L. Phillips, *Big Wayward Girl: An Informal Political History of California* (Garden City, N.Y.: Doubleday, 1968). To some extent in a class by itself is Carey McWilliams, *California: The Great Exception* (Santa Barbara, Calif.: Peregrine Smith, 1976, originally 1949). Major studies by political scientists are Dean R. Cresap, *Party Politics in the Golden State* (Los Angeles: Haynes Foundation, 1954); Winston W. Crouch *et al., California Government and Politics* (5th ed., Englewood Cliffs, N.J.: Prentice-Hall, 1972); David Farrelly and Ivan Hinderaker, eds., *The Politics of California: A Book of Readings* (New York: Ronald Press, 1951); Joseph P. Harris, *California Politics* (4th ed., San Francisco: Chandler, 1967); Bernard Hyink *et al., Politics and Government in California* (9th ed., New York: Crowell, 1975).

Periodicals

There are four major journals which every student of modern California politics can consult continuously with profit. *California History* (formerly entitled *California Historical Quarterly* and earlier *California Historical Society Quarterly*) has many specialized and general articles, as does *Southern California Quarterly* (formerly named *Southern California Historical Society Quarterly*). The *Western Political Quarterly* has published articles on every election in the state between 1948 and 1972 as well as many other useful studies. Since its inception in 1970 the *California Journal* has become indispensable for every serious student of contemporary California politics.

Special Studies

In addition to the above, the following are works of particular pertinence to the main topics in this study.

Chapter One: Robert F. Hennings, "California Democratic Politics in the Period of Republican Ascendancy," *Pacific Historical Review,* XXXI (August 1962), 267-280; Gilman M. Ostrander, *The Prohibition Movement in California, 1848-1933* (Berkeley: University of California Press, 1957); Jackson K. Putnam, "The Persistence of Progressivism in the 1920s: The Case of California," *Pacific Historical Review,* XXXV (November 1966), 395-411.

Chapter Two: Thomas S. Barclay, "Reapportionment in California," *Pacific Historical Review,* V (June 1936), 93-129; Robert E. Burke, *Olson's New Deal for California* (Berkeley: University of California Press, 1953); Clarke A. Chambers, *California Farm Organizations... 1929-1941* (Berkeley: University of California Press, 1952); Erwin Cooper, *Aqueduct Empire* (Glendale, Calif.: Arthur H. Clark, 1968); Robert de Roos, *The Thirsty Land: The Story of the Central Valley Project* (Stanford, Calif.: Stanford University Press, 1970); Jackson K. Putnam, *Old-Age Politics in California: From Richardson to Reagan* (Stanford, Calif.: Stanford University Press, 1970); Arthur H. Samish and Bob Thomas, *The Secret Boss of California: The Life and High Times of Art Samish* (New York: Crown Publishers, 1971).

Chapter Three: Edward L. Barrett, *The Tenney Committee* (Ithaca, N.Y.: Cornell University Press, 1951); David P. Gardner, *The California Oath Controversy* (Berkeley: University of California Press, 1967); Richard B. Harvey, *Earl Warren: Governor of California* (Jericho, N.Y.: Exposition Press, 1969); Leo Katcher, *Earl Warren: A Political Biography* (New York: McGraw-Hill, 1967); Earl Warren, *The Memoirs of Earl Warren* (Garden City, N.Y.: Doubleday, 1977); John D. Weaver, *Earl Warren: The Man, the Court, the Era* (Boston: Little Brown, 1967).

Chapter Four: Charles G. Bell and Charles M. Price, *The First Term: A Study of Legislative Socialization* (Beverly Hills, Calif.: Sage Publications, 1975); Francis Carney, "The Rise of the Democratic Clubs in California," in Eagleton Institute of Practical Politics, *Cases on Party Organization* (New York: McGraw-Hill, 1963), 32-63; James Q. Wilson, *The Amateur Democrat* (Chicago: University of Chicago Press, 1962).

Chapter Five: Bill Boyarsky, *The Rise of Ronald Reagan* (New York: Random House, 1968); Edmund G. Brown and Bill Brown, *Reagan: The Political Chameleon* (New York: Praeger, 1976); Lou Cannon, *Ronnie and Jessie* (Garden City, N.Y.: Doubleday, 1969); Joseph Lewis, *What Makes Reagan Run?* (New York: McGraw-Hill, 1968); Ronald Reagan with Richard Hubler, *Where's the Rest of Me?* (New York: Duell, Sloan and Pearce, 1965); Kent Steffgen, *Here's the Rest of Him* (Reno, Nev.: Foresight Books, 1968).

Chapter Six: John C. Bollens and G. Robert Williams, *Jerry Brown in a Plain Brown Wrapper* (Pacific Palisades, Calif.: Palisades Publishers, 1978); John J. Fitzpatrick, "His Father's Son," *New West,* January 16, 1978, pp. 34-43; Mary E. Leary, *Phantom Politics* (Washington, D.C.: Public Affairs Press, 1977); J. D. Lorenz, *Jerry Brown: The Man on the White Horse* (Boston: Houghton Mifflin, 1978); Robert Pack, *Jerry Brown: The Philosopher Prince* (New York: Stein and Day, 1978); Ed Salzman, *Jerry Brown: High Priest and Low Politician* (Sacramento: California Journal Press, 1976).

INDEX